LEONARD S. MARCUS

Petrouchka, illustrated by Jane Kendall (1983)

Picture Books (1984)

An Épinal Album: Popular Prints from Nineteenth-Century France (editor, 1984)

Humor and Play in Children's Literature (editor, 1989)

Mother Goose's Little Misfortunes, illustrated by Amy Schwartz (editor, 1990)

Margaret Wise Brown: Awakened by the Moon (1992)

Lifelines: A Poetry Anthology (editor, 1994)

75 Years of Children's Book Week Posters (1994)

Morrow Junior Books: The First Fifty Years (1996)

The Making of Goodnight Moon: A Fiftieth Anniversary Retrospective (1997)

A Caldecott Celebration: Six Artists and Their Paths to the Caldecott Medal (1998)

Dear Genius: The Letters of Ursula Nordstrom (editor, 1998)

Author Talk (2000)

Side by Side: Five Favorite Picture Book Teams Go to Work (2001)

Ways of Telling: Conversations on the Art of the Picture Book (2002)

Storied City: A Children's Book Walking-Tour Guide to New York City (2003)

The Wand in the Word: Conversations with Writers of Fantasy (2006)

Oscar: The Big Adventure of a Little Sock Monkey, co-authored with Amy Schwartz; illustrated by Amy Schwartz (2006)

Pass It Down: Five Picture-Book Families Make Their Mark (2007)

A Caldecott Celebration: Seven Artists and Their Paths to the Caldecott Medal (2008)

Minders of Make-Believe: Idealists, Entrepreneurs, and the Shaping of American Children's Literature (2008)

Funny Business: Conversations with Writers of Comedy (2009)

The Annotated Phantom Tollbooth (editor, 2011)

Show Me a Story! Why Picture Books Matter (2012)

Listening for Madeleine: A Portrait of Madeleine L'Engle in Many Voices (2012)

Maurice Sendak: A Celebration of the Artist and His Work (editor, 2013)

Comics Confidential: Thirteen Graphic Novelists Talk Story, Craft, and Life Outside the Box (2016)

The Runaway Bunny: A 75th Anniversary Retrospective (2017)

Golden Legacy: The Story of Golden Books (2007/2017)

The Kairos Novels, by Madeleine L'Engle (editor, 2018)

Helen Oxenbury: A Life in Illustration (2019)

100 Years of Children's Book Week Posters (2019)

The ABC of It: Why Children's Books Matter (2019)

You Can't Say That!: Writers for Young People Talk about Censorship, Free Expression, and the Stories They Have to Tell (2021)

Pictured Worlds: Masterpieces of Children's Book Art by 101 Essential Illustrators from Around the World (2023)

Mr. Lincoln Sits for His Portrait: The Story of a Photograph that Became an American Icon (2023)

Leo Lionni: Storyteller, Artist, Designer, co-authored with Steven Heller, Annie Lionni, and Stephanie Haboush Plunkett (2024)

Earthrise: The Story of the Photograph that Changed the Way We See Our Planet (2025)

EARTHRISE

LEONARD S. MARCUS

EARTHRISE

THE STORY OF THE PHOTOGRAPH THAT CHANGED THE WAY WE SEE OUR PLANET

Farrar Straus Giroux
New York

Farrar Straus Giroux Books for Young Readers
An imprint of Macmillan Publishing Group, LLC
120 Broadway, New York, NY 10271 • mackids.com

Our books may be purchased in bulk for promotional, educational, or business use.
Please contact your local bookseller or the Macmillan Corporate and Premium Sales
Department at (800) 221-7945 ext. 5442 or by email at
MacmillanSpecialMarkets@macmillan.com.

Library of Congress Cataloging-in-Publication Data
Names: Marcus, Leonard S., 1950– author.
Title: Earthrise : the story of a photograph that changed the way we see
our planet / Leonard S. Marcus.
Description: First edition. | New York : Farrar Straus Giroux, 2025. |
Includes bibliographical references and index. | Audience: Ages 10–14. |Audience:
Grades 7–9. | Summary: "From renowned researcher and children's lit scholar
Leonard S. Marcus comes a middle-grade nonfiction book about the astonishing
photograph taken during the Apollo 8 mission that forever shifted the
way we view our planet"— Provided by publisher.
Identifiers: LCCN 2024013104 | ISBN 9780374392116 (hardcover)
Subjects: LCSH: Project Apollo (U.S.)—Juvenile literature. | Apollo 8
(Spacecraft)—Juvenile literature. | Space flight to the moon—Juvenile literature.
| Photographs—History—Juvenile literature. | Earth (Planet)—Photographs
from space—Juvenile literature.
Classification: LCC TL789.8.U6 A5539 2025 | DDC 525.022/2—dc23/
eng/20240624
LC record available at https://lccn.loc.gov/2024013104

First edition, 2025

Book design by L. Whitt
Printed in the United States of America by Lakeside Book Company,
Harrisonburg, Virginia
ISBN 978-0-374-39211-6

1   3   5   7   9   10   8   6   4   2

FRONTISPIECE: *EARTHRISE*, TAKEN BY *APOLLO 8* ASTRONAUT BILL ANDERS WHILE IN
LUNAR ORBIT ON CHRISTMAS EVE, 1968, FROM A DISTANCE OF 23,900 MILES FROM EARTH

IN MEMORY OF AMY SCHWARTZ—
SHINING LIGHT, BEAUTIFUL SPIRIT

CONTENTS

EARTHRISE

Earth is again seen on the lunar horizon in this shot captured seven months after Bill Anders photographed *Earthrise*. Astronaut Michael Collins snapped this photograph of the returning *Apollo 11* lunar lander, with astronauts Neil A. Armstrong and Edwin E. Aldrin Jr. onboard, from his post on the *Apollo 11* command module.

INTRODUCTION

"What is the news, good neighbor, I pray?"
"They say a balloon has gone up to the moon
And won't be back till a week from today."
—Traditional nursery rhyme

We came all this way to explore the Moon, and the most
important thing is that we discovered the Earth.
—Bill Anders, Apollo 8 *astronaut*

When people look back now at NASA's Project Apollo, most point to the July 1969 Moon landing by crew members of *Apollo 11* as the US space program's single greatest accomplishment. Were not the earlier Apollo missions just dress rehearsals leading up to that one spectacular achievement?

Actually, no, they were not.

Daring, risky, historic "firsts" in space travel had been realized by nearly every other crew during the months and years leading up to commander Neil Armstrong's "one giant leap for Mankind."

Seven months earlier, the astronauts of *Apollo 8* became the first humans to orbit the Moon and, in making their pathfinding 240,000-mile journey, the first humans ever to break free of the Earth's gravity and visit another world.

Among the hundreds of photographs *Apollo 8* brought back was one that changed the way people understand their place in the universe. It is an image of the Earth, not the Moon, and it

The Earth was photographed from the vicinity of the Moon by *Lunar Orbiter 1*, an uncrewed spacecraft launched on August 10, 1966. *Lunar Orbiter 1* was the first US vehicle to orbit the Moon. Its primary mission was to send back images of potential landing sites on the lunar surface. This photo of the Earth, made without the benefit of a human in control of the camera, looks like a rough draft of the iconic image captured two years later by *Apollo 8* astronaut Bill Anders.

was taken by astronaut Bill Anders as *Apollo 8* orbited the Moon on the morning of Christmas Eve, 1968.

Photographing the Earth was not on the astronauts' official agenda, but Anders and his crewmates had all been awestruck by the never-before-seen sight of the Earth rising over the Moon's horizon, and so Anders, the mission photographer, took the picture anyway. Almost from the moment it was first published, that photograph, which became known as *Earthrise*, has been prized as one of the American space program's most lasting achievements.

Some viewers of *Earthrise* were humbled by it; others were stirred to action by its clear depiction of the Earth as a small, fragile-looking, yet also dynamic object—or organism—drifting in space. Many viewers felt that an image of the "whole Earth" was one they had been waiting to see. It helped inspire Earth Day, which was first celebrated in 1970, and the environmental movement itself. *Earthrise* too was a "giant leap for Mankind."

This is the story of that extraordinary photograph: who took it, why, and how it became an image that changed the world.

During the fall of 1957, Americans were alarmed to learn that the Soviet Union had launched *Sputnik 1*, the first ever human-built satellite, into Earth's orbit. The success of *Sputnik* was seen as dramatic proof of Soviet prowess in space-age technology and an ominous sign that the world was fast becoming a more dangerous place.

1

THE RACE

On October 4, 1957, the Soviet Union surprised the world by sending the first artificial satellite into Earth orbit. The Soviets called their high-tech wonder—a sleek, silvery orb about the size of a beachball—Sputnik, Russian for "fellow traveler."

In the news photos flashed around the globe, the four slender antennae streaming from *Sputnik 1*'s sides bore a funny resemblance to a cat's whiskers. All in all, the satellite looked more like a shiny art object than a cutting-edge piece of space-age technology. It was not Sputnik's appearance, though, but the eerie *beep-beep*, *beep-beep* signal it beamed back to Earth that spooked ordinary Americans, millions of whom heard the electronic pulse on the evening news—or on their own shortwave radios.

Americans accustomed to thinking of their country as safe, secure, and far from the historical battlefields of Europe and Asia now realized that modern aerospace science and engineering were making their world a much smaller and more dangerous place.

Fans of science fiction were less surprised than most about the satellite that orbited the Earth every 96 minutes in elliptical loops high overhead, and some were more fascinated than frightened by it.

But whatever the feelings about Sputnik, one thing was sure: A 'space race' between the United States and its archrival, the Soviet Union, had begun!

How had the Soviet Union, a desperately poor country for much of the twentieth century, leapfrogged over the US in such a key area of technology? Was this proof that the Soviet Union's socialist government was somehow superior to America's democracy? Had the US grown overconfident or lazy in the years following the Allies' great victory in the Second World War? Had Soviet scientists received better university training or were they harder working or more patriotic than their American counterparts? And what about Soviet schoolchildren? Were they too growing up better informed about science than their American peers and with bigger dreams of exploring the solar system and beyond? If so, then perhaps the US was already well on its way to losing its place as the world's greatest power.

Less than a month after *Sputnik 1*, the Soviets scored again with the launch of a second, more impressive satellite. *Sputnik 2* not only surpassed its predecessor in size and weight; it was also the first space vehicle ever to place a passenger in Earth orbit. Riding on board the unpiloted 1,100-pound capsule was a "space dog" named Laika—Russian for "barker."

Laika rocketed skyward with a supply of food and water but no mechanism for returning her to Earth. A tangle of sensors attached to her body allowed technicians on the ground to monitor her vital signs. An onboard television camera gave scientists close-up views of the dog's every movement. Although a malfunction of the capsule's temperature controls caused Laika's death much sooner than anticipated, the data scientists collected was enough to convince them that humans were indeed fit for space travel.

POOR LΛIKΛ!

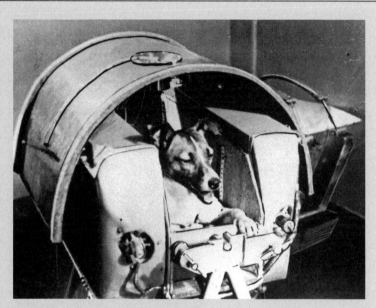

Once a stray dog wandering the streets of Moscow, Laika became the first animal to orbit the Earth during her flight aboard the Soviet *Sputnik 2* spacecraft, which blasted off on November 3, 1957. She is shown here in a mock cockpit.

Soviet scientists had mapped out a ten-day mission for the four-legged pioneer, a wiry-haired part-Samoyed terrier whose original name had been the less warriorlike Curly, but with no plan for bringing her back to Earth alive. News of the mission outraged the world's animal rights advocates, but the experiment suited Soviet scientists' needs perfectly. Before sending a human safely into space, researchers had to learn all they could about the physical stresses to be endured by their cosmonauts. Because dogs are genetically 95 percent identical to humans, observing the effects of space travel on the body of a canine seemed a promising approach, even if it meant sacrificing the dog.

The US military, meanwhile, was testing its own rockets but with discouragingly mixed results. In December 1957, the launchpad explosion at Florida's Cape Canaveral Air Force Station of the three-stage Redstone rocket attempting to carry a US satellite into orbit was reported in the press with sarcastic headlines like "Flopnik!" . . . "Oopsnik!" . . . and "Stayputnik!" In another uncrewed test, a Redstone rocket—originally designed as a warhead delivery system—barely lifted off the ground before settling back down on the launchpad in what became known derisively as the "four-inch flight."

Finally on January 31, 1958, the US, although still clearly behind the Soviets, managed to match *Sputnik 1* with an unmanned orbital communications satellite called *Explorer 1*. The satellite performed beautifully, prompting the US Army Ballistic Missile Agency to hastily schedule four follow-up launches for later that year. The plan backfired, however, when two of the new rockets crashed at liftoff.

With something obviously still very wrong about the US

EXPLORER 1

AMERICA'S FIRST EARTH SATELLITE

jpl

JET PROPULSION LABORATORY

CALIFORNIA INSTITUTE OF TECHNOLOGY

The US finally got into the space race with the successful launch of its first satellite on January 31, 1958. *Explorer 1* orbited the Earth every 118 minutes for nearly five months, collecting valuable information about radiation levels in space before burning up in the Earth's atmosphere in late May.

effort, Congress, on July 29, 1958, established the National Aeronautics and Space Administration, or NASA, as a civilian government agency to get to the bottom of the problem and take charge of nonmilitary American space research and exploration from then onward.

The world at mid-century looked to be a very scary place. During the Second World War, the US had formed the Allied coalition by joining forces with Great Britain and the Soviet Union and others to defeat an aggressive alliance of invading nations led by Germany and Japan known as the Axis powers. After the war, the US and Britain remained allies, but the Soviets broke with their partners, making their own intentions of world domination clear.

During what became known as the Cold War, the United States emerged as the universally acknowledged leader of the "free world" with the Soviet Union as its chief adversary. Now, as the US and the Soviets vied for the loyalty of the rest of the world's nations, Germany, Cuba, and China were just a few of the global flashpoints where a new "hot war," perhaps one involving nuclear

On April 9, 1959, NASA introduced its first astronaut class, the Mercury 7. Front row, left to right: Walter M. Schirra Jr., Donald K. "Deke" Slayton, John H. Glenn Jr., and M. Scott Carpenter; back row, Alan B. Shepard Jr., Virgil I. "Gus" Grissom, and L. Gordon Cooper Jr.

weapons, was viewed by many as a real possibility.

For a time, the space race seemed to drop out of the headlines, but when the next milestone event came nearly three years later, the news was very big news indeed—and once again it was all glory to the Soviets.

On April 12, 1961, an obscure Soviet air force pilot named Yuri Gagarin became the first human to travel in space. After orbiting the Earth once in a flight that lasted about two hours, this brave cosmonaut—as Soviet astronauts were known—initiated a planned, rapid descent and at

The son of farm workers, Yuri Alekseyevich Gagarin became the first human in space in the spring of 1961, as the pilot of the Soviet Union's *Vostok 1* spacecraft, in which he circled the globe once before returning to Earth 108 minutes later. A modest, likeable man who was deeply respected by his peers, Gagarin spent the rest of his short life as a national hero and worldwide celebrity. He died in March 1968 in a plane crash during a routine training flight.

four miles above the Earth's surface ejected from his *Vostok 1* space capsule, parachuting to safety.

He landed in the Soviet republic of Kazakhstan, nearly four hundred miles off target, in a potato field, where the first people to greet him were an elderly peasant farmer and her five-year-old granddaughter. Neither had the slightest idea who their strangely clad visitor might be, and it took Gagarin's soon-to-be famous toothy grin and a few reassuring words spoken in Russian to convince the pair that he was not some fantastic creature from an alien world: "I told them, don't be afraid, I am a Soviet citizen like you, who has descended from space."

As they chatted, Gagarin himself grew increasingly agitated, however. Because he had not been outfitted with a radio capable of ground-to-ground communication, he had no way to immediately notify Soviet space officials of his survival and was anxious to do so as soon as possible. There was nothing else for the world's first space traveler to do but ask his new best friends where he might find the nearest telephone.

It took just three weeks for the US to respond to *Vostok 1* with a manned mission of its own, albeit one that seemed a bit puny by comparison. Commander Alan Shepard blasted off from Cape Canaveral, Florida, on May 5, 1961, on a flight that lasted just fifteen minutes and took him on an arching, suborbital ride from the Cape to a designated splashdown point three hundred miles out in the Atlantic.

Shepard's flight aboard *Freedom 7* was over almost before it began, and he was reportedly furious not to have beaten the Soviets to the punch. But the news of his success was good enough to persuade the new president of the United States, John F. Kennedy, that the time was right to make an announcement calculated to turn the space race on its head and give Americans a thrilling goal they could all feel they shared.

Young and confident with movie-star good looks, Kennedy entered the White House at the start of 1961, succeeding Dwight

Fresh from his historic suborbital *Freedom 7* flight, astronaut Alan Shepard visited the White House on May 8, 1961, to receive NASA's Distinguished Service Medal from President John F. Kennedy. Standing beside the president are First Lady Jacqueline Kennedy and Vice President Lyndon B. Johnson.

D. Eisenhower—a former general and war hero who was old enough to be his father. Kennedy often spoke about the new generation he symbolized and whose turn it now was to lead, and about life as a glorious adventure, the time for which was also *now*.

Growing up as one of nine children in a colorful, wealthy Boston political family, Kennedy had loved reading about the heroic adventures of King Arthur and the Knights of the Round Table. Later, as a naval officer stationed in the Pacific during the Second World War, he won two medals including a Purple Heart for injuries received in the call of duty. Now as president,

Kennedy urged Americans to join him as fellow adventurers in exploring what he called the New Frontier.

Unlike the American prairie or California gold country of past generations, however, the frontier Kennedy had in mind was not necessarily an actual destination. The frontier he spoke about was more like an idea, or rather a series of ideas for solving some of the world's intractable problems: a plan, say, for ending hunger or poverty or the threat of nuclear war.

Kennedy had a talent for grand flourishes and he soon had patriotic American schoolchildren running fifty-yard dashes as part of his youth fitness program, and idealistic college graduates shipping off to all corners of the so-called underdeveloped world as volunteers in America's Peace Corps.

Barely four months into his presidency, however, the president went before Congress on May 25, 1961, to deliver a speech about his top priorities, and surprised many by suggesting that the New Frontier *was* a real place after all, and that that place was the Moon! The United States, he said, should commit itself, "before this decade is out," to "landing a man on the Moon and returning him safely to the Earth." This was a jaw-dropping idea.

Some NASA officials did not believe the young president was serious, and many doubted the deadline he had just set for them could possibly be met. As Kennedy himself acknowledged, a rocket big and powerful enough to carry out a Moon mission did not yet exist. Such a rocket would have to be made in part of special materials that had yet to be invented—materials capable of withstanding temperatures far greater than any previously recorded on Earth. Oh, yes, and the price tag would be . . . astronomical.

Opinion polls showed that fewer than fifty percent of Americans believed a Moon mission was worth the trouble, danger, or expense. Kennedy knew that to win support for the huge, costly project, it would not be enough to appeal to Americans' hopes and dreams; he would also have to play on their fears. If the Soviets reached the Moon first, what might they do militarily with all the advanced technologies they were sure to develop along the way? Did Americans really want to take the chance of finding out?

In a world in which the two chief rival nations already had large stockpiles of nuclear weapons, it was not hard to imagine truly hair-raising answers to that question.

On February 20, 1962, to mark the success that same morning of astronaut John Glenn's orbital flight—a first for the lagging US space program—the United States Postal Service announced the release of a commemorative stamp depicting Glenn's *Project Mercury* space capsule.

2

VISION AND TRAGEDY

"We choose to go to the Moon," President Kennedy said in a September 1962 speech at Rice University in Texas. "We choose to go to the Moon in this decade and do the other things, not because they are easy, but because they are hard, because that goal will serve to organize and measure the best of our energies and skills, because that challenge is one that we are willing to accept, one we are unwilling to postpone, and one which we intend to win."

Once President Kennedy secured the funding NASA needed, the agency went into overdrive to map out a plan for making his man-on-the-moon mission more than just a pie-in-the-sky dream. Kennedy's announcement had

In September 1962, President Kennedy visited the NASA Space Center in Houston. Here he is seen inspecting an early model of the Apollo command module with the Center's director, Dr. Robert R. Gilruth, serving as his guide.

also put the Soviets under great pressure to accelerate their efforts to achieve the same goal; as a result, the pace of the Soviet-US competition ticked upward rapidly.

On August 6, 1961, the Soviets sent a second cosmonaut into Earth orbit, this time for a full day—setting a new endurance record. Then on August 11 and 12 of the following year, they launched back-to-back multiday orbital missions, and another two missions in rapid succession in June 1963.* Crewed NASA space missions also became routine occurrences. In a refreshing change for the American side, flawless performances by man and machine also became the norm.

At first a geeky, little-known government research arm, NASA morphed almost overnight into a high-profile, supercool New Frontier operation staffed by whip-smart rocket scientists and clean-cut, highly trained All-American space cowboys.

Getting the public, including schoolchildren, excited about space exploration became a major NASA priority, and before long, signs of success were to be observed in the soaring demand for toy rockets at Christmastime; the faddish popularity of an orange-flavored, powdered breakfast drink called Tang, which the astronauts were said to take along on every mission; and the regular appearance in dinner-table conversation of NASA catchwords like "A-OK" (for anything that was going as planned) and

---

*Vostok 6, a Soviet orbital mission launched on June 16, 1963, made history as the first space flight piloted by a woman, twenty-six-year-old cosmonaut Valentina Tereshkova.

Space-themed playgrounds, toys, and games proliferated during the 1960s in the US and beyond. NASA built this futuristic play park on the grounds of its Manned Spacecraft Center in Houston.

"glitch" (for anything that wasn't). New TV shows like *Lost in Space* and *Star Trek* vied for top ratings with *Gunsmoke* and other oldfangled Westerns. For Americans of all ages, the astronauts were fast becoming folk heroes to put beside Lewis and Clark, Annie Oakley, and Davy Crockett—and media celebrities whose faces were known to everyone from the TV news and pages of Americans' favorite magazines.

Like it or not, astronauts had to adjust to life in the limelight and make the best of the loss of privacy that went with their new public roles. *Life* magazine—a photo-filled newsweekly read by millions—contracted with NASA to grant its reporters and photographers regular access not only to the astronauts themselves but also to their families and homes. *Life* paid the astronauts handsomely for the privilege, effectively doubling their

This popular Little Golden Book, written by Rose Wyler and illustrated by Tibor Gergely, was published in 1958—the year NASA was created.

modest government salaries, but it came at a price, especially for the astronauts' families and most of all for their wives.

Astronaut wives were expected always to look their best, to smile for the photographers' cameras, have an upbeat comment for reporters at the tip of their tongues—and keep their worries and fears to themselves. It was impossible *never* to worry, of course, knowing as they did that any astronaut, no matter how physically fit or talented or experienced, might die on any given day in a freak training accident or on an actual mission.

Astronaut Frank Borman flew on two orbital Gemini flights prior to commanding the crew of *Apollo 8*. When Borman's wife, Susan, traveled to Cape Kennedy to witness the launch of one of these earlier missions, a *Life* photographer caught her turning away at the very moment of lift-off with an unmistakable look of terror on her face. In the days following publication of that photograph, Susan Borman was widely mocked for having let down her guard and shown the world what critics called her weakness. Much to her credit, Borman stood her ground, and explained her reaction in an article about what it was really like to live in a fishbowl while facing so much danger *and* trying to hold a family together. Her first-person opinion piece was reprinted in newspapers nationwide: "These past weeks I have worn my heart on my sleeve. Some people say that they were glad

The Bormans (Susan, foreground; rear from left, sons Frederick, Edwin, and their famous dad) are pictured here as they prepare to leave on a 1969 European goodwill trip on behalf of the US government. As Susan Borman recalled of life in the NASA spotlight: "It wasn't discussed, it wasn't written, but . . . you had better to be . . . the all-American family in everything you say and do! We kept it like *Leave It to Beaver*."

Susan Borman, wife of astronaut Frank Borman, embraces her sons during the *Gemini 7* launch on December 4, 1965. This widely circulated photograph, in which the two young boys gaze upward in amazement while their mother turns away in fear, gave the public a rare glimpse of the emotional stresses under which the astronauts' wives lived constantly.

to see an astronaut's wife willing to admit that she was scared. Others were unhappy that I didn't maintain a stiff upper lip. At one time the criticism would have cut me deeply. I have since realized that you can't be all things to all people, so I decided not to pretend. I decided to be myself. I am just a woman who loves her husband and wants him to be safe."

The astronauts and their families all lived in contemporary, split-level homes in Timber Cove, Texas, a picture-postcard suburb thirty miles southeast of downtown Houston. The wives were a tight-knit group, many having first met during their husbands' test-pilot days. More than a few had attended the same funerals of test-pilot friends who did not come home one evening from their thrilling but deadly serious jobs. The wives comforted each other as they wondered in private whose husband would be next.

Even apart from the obvious risks, astronaut life was far from ordinary, involving as it did high-stress training exercises, long workdays, and frequent travel to work sites far from home. Bill Anders, an astronaut who cared deeply about being a good father, estimated that during intensive training periods, he typically had no more than eleven minutes per week to devote to each of his five children. It should have surprised nobody that several astronauts' marriages did not survive the strain.

The astronauts (and to a lesser extent their families) also enjoyed some enviable perks of course: special deals on sports cars (for a time nearly every astronaut drove a Corvette); VIP travel across the US and around the globe; invitations to party with all manner of celebrities and to meet with high-ranking government officials from the president on down; rare access to the world's most advanced technologies; and the chance to inspire an entire generation of young people. For most members of the astronaut corps, the best perk of all was the opportunity of a lifetime to play a pivotal role in a history-making adventure.

By November 1963, NASA had recruited three groups of astronauts, for a total of twenty-nine. Far from the diverse group the astronaut corps would later become, all twenty-nine were white, Christian men in their thirties.* All but one were married;

---

*In 1959, NASA physician William Randolph Lovelace II launched a privately funded project to identify and train a small group of women capable of joining the astronaut corps. Lovelace's work showed that the "Mercury 13," as the women who successfully completed the training program came to be

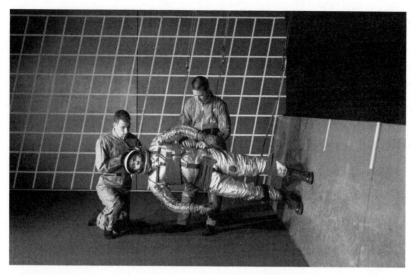

NASA devised a number of ingenious ways to prepare the astronauts for the novel aspects of life in space. This photo from 1963 depicts a device for giving future space travelers an approximation of the experience of operating in reduced-gravity conditions.

astronaut families had an average of two young children. Nearly all had military backgrounds, and all had advanced flying experience, a record of exceptional personal fitness and health, and degrees in science or engineering.

Some astronauts were a lot more outgoing than others, but deep down they were a like-minded group whose members shared strong character traits not always found in the same individual. Not surprisingly, only applicants who were intensely driven and competitive ever made the final cut and entered the

known, were as well suited as the men NASA was selecting to crew its space missions, if not more so. Unfortunately, NASA officials ignored Lovelace's findings and did not send an American woman astronaut into space until 1983, when Sally Ride was chosen for the crew of the Space Shuttle *Challenger*.

astronaut corps. But they also had to be fiercely loyal team players and capable of setting aside their ego in a pinch.

NASA's master plan had been designed in three phases of increasing complexity. As the program progressed from the solo flights of Mercury (1961–1963) to the two-man Gemini missions (1964–1966), and then to the three-man Apollo missions (1967–1972), team spirit counted for more and more. By the spring of 1963, when astronaut L. Gordon Cooper sailed through the marathon 22-orbit, 34-hour mission that brought the Mercury series to a triumphant close, the astronaut corps had more than proven its worth, and NASA appeared to be on track to meet President Kennedy's end-of-decade deadline.

Then something unimaginable happened. In the early afternoon of November 22, 1963, while campaigning for reelection in Texas, President Kennedy was shot and killed—assassinated—as he rode in an open car in a sunlit motorcade through the streets of Dallas.

The terrible violence of that day shocked the world and left the US with a new president few Americans knew much about. Lyndon Johnson was a Texan and, as Washington insiders had long since learned, an exceptionally artful dealmaker. Before becoming the vice president under Kennedy, Johnson had reigned for years as the single most powerful member of the United States Senate. It was not by chance that NASA had chosen Houston, Texas, in Johnson's home state, as the site for its massive new Space Center. Johnson had fought hard for NASA from its very beginnings; if

Just over one hour after the news of President Kennedy's death was announced to the world, Lyndon Baines Johnson took the oath of office as the thirty-sixth president of the United States. To signal that the operations of the US government had not been disrupted by the tragedy in Dallas, Johnson was anxious to be sworn in as quickly as possible and took the oath on Air Force One shortly before he and his entourage took off for Washington. The media-savvy new president made certain the ceremony was captured by White House photographer Cecil Stoughton for all to see.

anything, he was an even bigger champion of the agency than Kennedy had been.

Now with Johnson as president, NASA was sure to have all the funding it would ever need. But that was not all. As one of his first presidential acts, he renamed Cape Canaveral "Cape Kennedy." From then on, Project Apollo was no longer just about beating the Soviets to the Moon. It had now also become a memorial to the president whose dream had done so much to inspire the nation.

NASA·S·65-893

A NASA artist's rendering of the interior of the two-person Gemini spacecraft in which astronauts carried out ten crewed missions between 1965 and 1966.

3

FASTER

With a clear signal to press ahead and with newfound purpose, NASA next completed all twelve of its scheduled Gemini flights—ten crewed and two uncrewed—between April 1964 and November 1966. Each mission was designed to answer some basic question or questions about the logistics of space travel, or to perfect a battery of skills and techniques essential for going to the Moon.

- *In the vastness of space, would it be possible for one vehicle to pull up alongside another and join snugly together like interlocking puzzle pieces, as the lunar lander and command module would need to do for the return flight to Earth? (The astronauts of* Gemini 7 *showed that it was.)*

- *Would the human body continue to function normally after a week—or two weeks—of continuous space travel in a weightless condition? (The answer, a resounding yes, was nailed down by the crew of* Gemini 7, *who*

*circled the Earth for 330 hours, or nearly 14 days—a
new space endurance record. This was welcome news
because the Moon landing mission would require only
8 days to complete.)*

- *Were humans capable of stepping out into space and
performing strenuous emergency repair work on the
CSM (or Command Service Module), or would even
the fittest astronaut become exhausted too quickly to
carry out such a task? (Gemini 12 showed that vigorous
manual work was in fact a possibility in space.)*

The first American spacewalk! The first in-flight vehicle docking! The first use of small onboard thruster rockets to micromanage a spacecraft's orbital path! All these firsts and many others were achieved during the Gemini years—an exciting, productive time at NASA.

And now finally: Apollo!

In contrast to the gloomy parade of exploding American rockets of the 1950s, Project Mercury had gone off almost entirely without a hitch—and without a single casualty; the crews of its successor program, Project Gemini, experienced at least two terrifying near-misses but had all come home alive, too.* NASA's practice of running duplicate missions to make

*The main objective of the *Gemini 8* mission was to master the techniques required for rendezvousing and docking with another vehicle in space. The docking maneuver went well, but an equipment failure caused the *Gemini 8* space capsule to start rolling and tumbling violently. The crew were in

Apollo 1 astronauts (from left to right) Gus Grissom, Edward White, and Roger Chaffee posing in front of Launch Complex 34, where their Saturn 1 launch vehicle was already in place nearly two months before their scheduled liftoff on February 21, 1967.

certain that the success of a given flight was itself not an accident, and its insistence on built-in redundancies, or backup systems, to reduce the chance of an in-flight equipment failure turning fatal, had clearly paid off.

Then, just as preparations for the first Apollo mission were nearing completion, tragedy struck. On January 27, 1967, less than one month before the scheduled launch of *Apollo 1*, a fire broke out at Cape Kennedy during a launch-site training session, killing all three astronauts assigned to the mission. The CSM

danger of blacking out and dying until Commander Neil Armstrong finally found a way to correct the problem. (His lifesaving action may have cemented his selection as commander of the *Apollo 11* mission during which he became the first human to walk on the Moon.) Later, *Gemini 9* astronaut Gene Cernan became overheated and exhausted during a spacewalk as he struggled to return to the space capsule. This prompted changes in capsule design and astronaut training that made later "extra-vehicular activities" both safer and less physically demanding.

had been mounted in place atop the Saturn 1B rocket that was to propel the crew of three into a low Earth orbit, where their job was to have been to put the space capsule through its first battery of rigorous in-flight tests. The astronauts had suited up and strapped themselves into their couches as if for liftoff when without warning a flash fire triggered by an electrical spark erupted inside the cramped and oxygen-rich compartment, whose hatch had been

The burned-out *Apollo 1* command module still sat atop its Saturn 1B rocket at Launch Complex 34, a day after the tragic fire in which all three astronauts perished.

locked, making a rapid escape impossible. All three men were trapped inside and died before rescuers could pull them to safety.

Shaken and horrified, NASA officials immediately opened an investigation that led to a top-to-bottom redesign of the module and everything associated with it. As terrible as the accident was, however, those in charge continued to take the classic engineers' view that every technical problem had a technical solution.

While the effort to rethink Apollo was sure to affect the project's timeline, no one spoke—at least not openly—about abandoning the project altogether or extending the moon land-

The German-born von Braun led the design team that created the Saturn V rocket. Highly regarded as an engineer, in the US he became a figure of considerable controversy because of his earlier work in rocket technology for the German Nazi regime during the Second World War.

ing deadline past 1969. NASA officials remained tight-lipped and determined. Now that this problem had arisen, the team would simply not stop until they had fixed it.

But time was running out.

The original Apollo plan called for twenty missions in all. First up was to have been the ill-fated *Apollo 1* Earth-orbital flight, followed by *Apollos 2* through *6*, all uncrewed missions for road-testing the Saturn V rocket and other key Moon mission components.

Following the fire, however, NASA retired the flight

Thought by some at NASA to resemble a bug, this 1963 model represents an early prototype of the Apollo lunar lander.

designation *Apollo 1* altogether and postponed the first crewed flight until much later in the sequence. As part of the same streamlining effort, NASA also eliminated *Apollos 2* and *3*. This left *Apollo 4* as the first mission in the series. *Apollos 4* and *6* now became the long-awaited initial trials of Saturn V. NASA was betting heavily on the brand-new giant rocket that chief engineer Wernher von Braun considered his masterpiece.

The uncrewed *Apollo 4* test flight went well but the Saturn rocket's performance for *Apollo 6*, which was also uncrewed, was a lot less reassuring. This time, the three-stage rocket experienced engine failures in both its second and third stages. It was only because the booster had been so artfully designed that the combined efforts of ground engineers and the Saturn V's onboard guidance system were able to maneuver the CSM back to Earth intact, thereby salvaging a substantial portion of the mission.

Although a final round of design tweaks was certainly in order, NASA's overall verdict on Saturn V came out positive. In NASA-speak, the Saturn V was now "human rated"—good to go with a crew.

But what about the CSM that the astronauts would ride to the Moon? *Apollo 7*'s crewed, Earth-orbital mission, launched with a smaller Saturn 1B rocket on October 11, was to be a critical test of that vital component, which had undergone numerous design changes in the wake of the fire that claimed the lives of the *Apollo 1* astronauts.

As important as that goal was in and of itself, NASA had also decided to make the outcome of that nearly eleven-day flight the basis for determining how best to use the little time that remained before the clock ran out on President Kennedy's end-of-the-decade pledge. Even a partial mission failure would almost certainly end all hope of meeting the goal. But a success would set in motion a daring new plan that NASA had secretly devised over the summer.

At NASA, the summer of 1968 had been a time for stock-taking, much like the one after the *Apollo 1* fire. Not only was the Saturn V rocket behind schedule; so was the Lunar Module (or LM, pronounced "lem"). As these setbacks became increasingly worrisome, NASA quietly opted to reassign the *Apollo 8* crew (one of whose main jobs was to test the LM) to the later *Apollo 9* slot, and to move the original *Apollo 9* crew up a slot as the new *Apollo 8* team, with a scheduled launch date sometime in December.

The change was more than a simple crew-and-mission swap, however. The newly designated *Apollo 8* team, Frank Borman, Michael Collins, and Bill Anders, were to carry out a mission very different from the one they had been training for. The new mission would be far more complex—and dangerous. Adding further to the challenge, the astronauts would have only four months to prepare for it, a fraction of the usual time. And there was one more thing: If *Apollo 7* revealed any major defects in the CSM's design or performance, *Apollo 8* might be postponed or canceled altogether.

Under the old plan, Borman, Collins, and Anders were to have maneuvered their spacecraft into a "parking" Earth orbit that enabled them to coast around the planet as they conducted advanced tests of the CSM and LM. At no time would their travels take them more than four thousand miles from Earth. Much of their training took place at the North American Aviation company's Downey, California, headquarters, where the CSM was being built, and a special flight simulator had been constructed to allow the astronauts to rehearse their flight plan, like actors preparing for a play. Each time the crew made a serious error while flying the simulator, a ground technician would inform them that they had just crashed the CSM and died.

That summer, Michael Collins developed a painful bone spur that required surgery and necessitated his being dropped from the crew. Collins was reassigned to the role of Capcomm (short for Capsule Communicator) for *Apollo 8*, the astronaut on the ground who maintained regular radio contact with the crew.* James Lovell became the mission's new command module pilot.

That August, the *Apollo 8* crew were in Downey when Borman was pulled away from a training session to take a phone call from Houston. On the line was Deke Slayton, the former astronaut who now directed NASA flight crew operations and as such was the astronauts' boss. It was Slayton who handpicked every Apollo crew and backup team and was responsible for their training. He sounded on edge as he told Borman to drop whatever he was doing and get back to the Houston Space Center immediately.

Borman, however, was intent on completing the simulator session and, turning a bit testy, said as much to Slayton. Anyway, why couldn't Slayton just give him the big news over the phone?

Now NASA's operations director became impatient.

"Dammit, Borman . . . this is classified!" he growled, before signing off with a direct order to "grab an airplane now!"

In Houston, Slayton brought Borman up to speed. He detailed NASA's anxious late-night, back-of-the-envelope calculations and mission reshuffle—its last-ditch effort to keep the Moon landing on track. Borman, Lovell, and Anders would remain together as a team. Now, however, achieving Earth orbit would be the least of their objectives. Traveling at the

---

*On July 16, 1969, Collins finally blasted off for the Moon as the command module pilot of the crew of *Apollo 11*.

From left to right, *Apollo 7* astronauts Walter M. Schirra Jr., Donn F. Eisele, and Walter Cunningham practice splashdown procedure in the Gulf of Mexico.

record-breaking velocity of more than twenty-four thousand miles an hour, they would fly nearly one quarter of a million miles to come within seventy miles of the lunar surface and become the first humans to insert themselves in lunar orbit.

No member of the crew would set foot on the Moon but they would all come closer by far to the Earth's nearest neighbor than had anyone before them. While in lunar orbit, they would also become the first humans to view the Moon's dark side. If something went terribly wrong, they might never return; in that case, they would become the first humans to be lost in space.

NASA made its plans for the daring mission public on August 19, 1968, as the *Apollo 8* crew began training in earnest for the strange journey that—if all went well for *Apollo 7*—lay ahead of them.

4

ROCKET MEN

With so much at stake, tensions at NASA were already running high in mid-October 1968 when officials in Houston received an alarming top-secret memorandum from the Central Intelligence Agency. *Apollo 7* was circling the Earth just then, and the mission was going well. But now Houston learned that the Soviets were planning their own Moon shot before the end of the year.*

This news made the outcome of the current mission more critical than ever. *Apollo 7*'s routine splashdown on October 22 was the green light Borman and his crew had been waiting for. The final leg of the race to the Moon was about to begin.

Frank Borman was an ideal choice to command the new *Apollo 8* mission. It was not just his long experience as a test pilot that made him right for the risky assignment. Over the past year, he had had a leading role in the no-holds-barred investigation

---

*The Soviet space program had suffered a major setback in April 1967 when Colonel Vladimir Komarov, the cosmonaut piloting an Earth-orbital mission in *Soyuz 1*, died during reentry after the capsule's parachutes failed to deploy. By mid-1968, the Soviets still had not tested their equivalent of the Saturn V Moon rocket and, like the Americans, were engaged in a desperate game of catchup.

The members of the original *Apollo 8* crew were, from left to right, William Anders, Michael Collins, and Frank Borman.

into the *Apollo 1* tragedy and in the major redesign that ensued. Borman probably knew as much as anyone about how the CSM worked, what could go wrong with it, and in case of emergency, what could be done to fix it.

Born in Gary, Indiana, and raised in Tucson, Arizona, Frank Borman had loved to fly ever since his father treated him to a ride in an old-fashioned open-air biplane when he was just five years old. By fifteen, young Frank had earned his pilot's license and decided that flying would play a big part in his future.

At school, he was known as a smart, driven, decisive, and at times insufferably bossy young man: a perfectionist who had no patience for the imperfections of others. On graduating from high

Military test pilots Frank Borman and Jim Lovell got to fly the world's most advanced planes, like those from the 1950s pictured here at Edwards Air Force Base, California. The work was considered dangerous but also thrilling by those who were willing to take the risk.

school, he enrolled at West Point, where he thrived in the military academy's discipline- and mission-driven culture. From there he entered the Air Force, first as a fighter pilot and then as a test pilot. For a fearless flyer like him, the latter assignment was the most coveted one of all, as it put him at the controls of the world's most advanced excprimental flying machines—with a license to press them to the absolute limit of their performance potential.

More than a few of Borman's colleagues died on the job as they pushed the envelope of the latest untried aircraft a bit too far while vying to set the next world speed or altitude record. The test pilot's life was not for the timid, and Borman loved being a member of such an elite corps of professional risk-takers. Another reason that military life appealed so strongly to him was that he considered himself a diehard Cold Warrior. Borman joined NASA with the number-one goal of making certain the US, not the Soviet Union, came out on top in the race to the Moon. He claimed not to care all that much about whether he personally set foot on the lunar surface, just so long as the first human to do so was an American.

Borman firmly believed he was one of NASA's all-around best astronauts and didn't mind saying so. For those who took this as a sign of a swelled head it must have been amusing to learn that his oddly box-shaped, extra-large actual head was the only one too big to fit inside the Apollo astronauts' standard-issue space helmet, which resembled an inverted fishbowl. A special helmet had to be made just for him.

Fellow crew member Jim Lovell was as easygoing as Borman was earnest. He had grown up in the Midwest reading H. G. Wells's *The Time Machine* and Jules Verne's *From the Earth to the Moon*, and as a high schooler had teamed up with friends to build homemade rockets for fun. Young Lovell looked up to American rocket engineer Robert Goddard as a hero, the more so because when skeptics ridiculed Goddard's revolutionary ideas about rocket design, he had pressed on with his work anyway, declaring in a famous 1920 letter to the *New York Times*: "Every vision is a joke until the first man accomplishes it; once realized, it becomes commonplace." Goddard designed and built the world's first liquid-fuel rocket and devised the first multistage rocket, breakthrough concepts that later proved critical to the realization of crewed space projects like those undertaken by NASA.

While still in high school, Lovell sought career advice from the American Rocket Society. His family, however, could not afford to send him to one of the top-rated engineering schools the Society recommended, so he enrolled in the US Naval Academy instead,

L'instrument monté. (Page 80.)

Une heure. (Page 154.)

Le soleil... (Page 127.)

In some ways, French science fiction writer Jules Verne (1828–1905) did an astonishing job in *From the Earth to the Moon* and its sequel, *Round the Moon* (both published 1865), of imagining how a trip to the Moon might unfold. Verne even pinpointed Florida as the probable launch site. But he missed the mark on other key details, envisioning a giant cannon as the launch mechanism and a command module whose interior décor, as depicted here by illustrator Émile-Antoine Bayard, bore an oddly close resemblance to a well-furnished Victorian parlor.

and afterward spent four years as a Navy test pilot before joining NASA in 1962 as a member of the second group of astronauts. Lovell was no less dedicated a military man than Borman, but his reason for joining the astronaut corps was not the same: For him, signing on with NASA was all about the adventure.

Prior to *Apollo 8*, Lovell had flown in two Gemini Earth-orbital missions, logging a total of eighteen days in space, hands down the world's record until then. His crewmate for the earlier of the two flights, the thirteen-day *Gemini 7* mission, had been none other than Frank Borman, whom some at NASA had initially thought might not be the best companion for him given their contrasting personalities. Would no-nonsense Borman and laid-back Lovell still be on speaking terms after nearly two weeks of being scrunched together in a vehicle half the size of a Volkswagen Beetle?

Officially, the marathon mission had been designed to test the astronauts' *physical* stamina. But had NASA scientists secretly conspired to measure their psychological endurance as well? Until then, doctors were not sure how the human heart and circulatory system would fare in a weightless environment, where the steady flow of blood, so vital for life, had to proceed unaided by the downward pull of gravity. *Gemini 7* would show conclusively that the human body was quite adaptable in this and other ways. As for Borman and Lovell's personal chemistry, on learning they both had a soft spot for country music, the two men got along like a house on fire and whiled away their downtime crooning their favorite songs. After splashdown and upon reemerging in public on the deck of the aircraft carrier USS *Wasp*, Lovell teased the assembled press corps with the "news" that he and Borman wished to announce their engagement.

As *Apollo 8*'s flight navigator, Lovell was responsible for keeping the astronauts on course. Naturally, NASA had the latest computers for guiding and tracking every phase of the mission. But the planners in Houston lived in dread of a technological glitch—yes, glitch!—that could leave the crew hopelessly stranded. What if a sudden loss of onboard power severed all communication with the ground? Without a reliable backup, the astronauts would be left to fend for themselves, cut off from Earth and everyone on it in a way that no human had ever before experienced.

NASA engineers generally favored the latest technologies, but in this instance mission planners had opted for a decidedly low-tech backup, training Lovell in the centuries-old practice of navigating by the stars.

STEERING BY THE HEAVENS

"Celestial navigation" is the name for a wayfinding technique first developed in the 1700s as an aid to British mariners at sea. It entails the use of a comparatively low-tech device called a sextant, the purpose of which is to determine a traveler's location by plotting the positions of a few known stars or other heavenly bodies relative to one another and the horizon line. By determining the relative locations of

A ship's captain using a modern, hand-held sextant to plot his position at sea

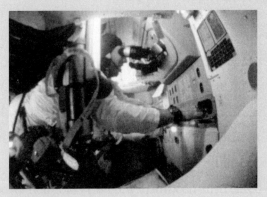

Jim Lovell peers into a state-of-the-art sextant at the *Apollo 8* command module's guidance and navigation station.

each star in such a group—NASA had selected thirty-seven stars for Lovell to know by sight based on their brightness and location—the Apollo craft's own position could then be calculated. Lovell's sextant came equipped with two built-in, high-power telescopes, but it was not otherwise much different in design from those used by eighteenth-century seafaring explorers like James Cook and George Vancouver.

Lovell might only be called upon to use his star-gazing skills in the event of an emergency, but if that were to happen, he was as good a man as any for the job. Famously cool under pressure, Lovell, back in his test-pilot days, had earned his colleagues' respect, and the nickname "Shaky" for being one of the most *un*shakable individuals they had ever come across—high praise indeed from a group of seasoned test pilots.

Unofficially, Lovell was also *Apollo 8*'s onboard comedian. He liked to repeat a favorite astronaut one-liner: "How does it feel to sit atop a vehicle built by the lowest bidder?" On the early morning of December 21, as he prepared to wriggle into the cramped command module where his crewmates had already settled into place, Lovell took a moment to gaze down at the Florida landscape still shrouded in darkness and said in mock disbelief to anyone who might be listening, "These NASA people are serious. They're going to send us to the Moon. My God, we really are doing this."

The third crew member was mission systems engineer Bill Anders. Anders's main job was to know all about the 566 switches and dozens of lights and instruments arrayed within the command module and to master the inner workings of every onboard system—from the electrical wiring and oxygen supply to the audio center and plumbing. Anders had previously made a special study of the LM. But because the lunar landing craft did not figure in the revised mission, planners had also designated him *Apollo 8*'s photographer.

Earnest, quick, and doggedly task-oriented, Anders struck

colleagues as a younger Frank Borman, apart from the fact that he was modest to a fault. At 5'8", he was a bit shorter than his crewmates and was the only one of the three who had not been a test pilot or flown on a previous NASA mission. But Anders's credentials were rock-solid in other ways. Born in British Hong Kong, he was the son of a decorated Navy officer who had performed heroically in battle while defending American interests in Asia during the second Sino-Japanese War. From childhood, he had

Apollo 8 astronauts (from left) Frank Borman, Jim Lovell, and Bill Anders appear relaxed as their mission's Saturn V rocket inches forward atop a jumbo crawler-transporter from the Vehicle Assembly Building at Cape Kennedy to Launch Complex 39A.

known he was bound for a life in the military. After the Anders family returned to the States, young Bill came into his own as a quiet, studious teenager with a wide range of interests that included mineralogy, wilderness hiking and fishing, the study of snakes, and—after his father, like Borman's, treated him to a joyride on an old-fashioned biplane—flying.

As a young reader, Anders favored science books and true stories about seafarers and other adventurers. On graduating from the Naval Academy, he joined the Air Force as a fighter pilot and was soon given the awesome responsibility of flying jets armed with nuclear warheads. Performing this nerve-racking task at supersonic speeds and occasionally even coming face-to-face in mid-air with his Soviet counterparts required a special set of personality traits and skills, among them extraordinary discipline and decisiveness and the ability to communicate precisely enough to prevent a potentially catastrophic misunderstanding.

While in the Air Force, Anders earned an advanced degree in nuclear engineering, a credential that helped win him a place in the astronaut corps but may also have marked him as the kind of astronaut who was less likely to walk on the Moon than be assigned to remain onboard the orbiting CSM to make certain that all was in working order for the return to Earth. Regardless of whether he walked on the Moon, however, Anders, like Lovell, saw his job first and foremost as a great adventure.

5

THE NUMBERS

Not everyone at NASA was convinced that four months was enough time for the crew to train properly, or that making the very first crewed flight of a Saturn V rocket a Moon mission was a risk worth taking.

The Saturn V was by far the largest, most powerful, and most complex rocket ever built. People at NASA had their favorite pet names for it, names like "Magnificent Beast" and "Monster." It stood as tall as a thirty-six-story building and nearly as high as the tallest redwood tree. It was fifty-eight feet taller than the Statue of Liberty. Perched on its launchpad, it was just a bit taller than a football field is long.

A rocket, essentially, is a self-propelled explosive device designed to release its energy in a highly concentrated and precisely focused burst of thrust. The Saturn V had five jumbo engines arrayed at its base, each capable of generating more than one million pounds of thrust at liftoff. If all five engines fired on time and in the right sequence and continued to work as planned, the immense force they released would propel the 3,100-ton rocket skyward. It would take the giant rocket twelve

The 138-foot-long Stage 1 column of the Saturn V rocket used in the *Apollo 8* mission is shown here being moved inside Cape Kennedy's cavernous Vehicle Assembly Building, supported by a crane capable of handling 175 tons, or the equivalent of twenty-plus elephants.

long seconds to clear the launch pad; but barely more than one minute later the Saturn V would break the sound barrier at an altitude of approximately five miles above the Earth's surface.

RISKY ODDS

A staggering 5.6 million individual parts went into the construction of the Saturn V, Apollo CSM, and related components. A total of 1.5 million systems, subsystems, and assemblies held the parts together and made them work. This meant that even if 99.9 percent of all the parts and systems

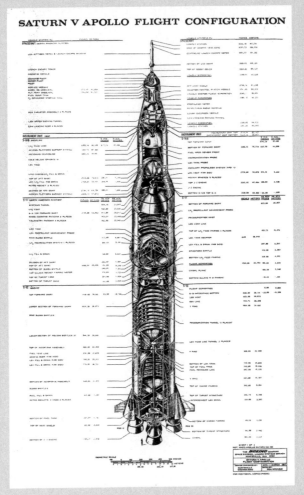

A schematic view of the interior of the Saturn V rocket
that only begins to suggest the complexity of its internal
construction and seamlessly integrated systems

functioned flawlessly, the chances of at least one failure
with potentially catastrophic consequences remained in the
thousands. The checkout procedures manual prepared for the
first Saturn V rocket took the form of a book that was 5,000

Film footage of the Saturn V at blastoff shows what looks like a huge fire raging underneath just as the rocket starts upward on its strangely drowsy initial ascent. This impression of course is a false one. The base of the rocket was constructed of one of the new materials that President Kennedy had envisioned: a special nickel-based superalloy capable of withstanding temperatures of up to 6000 degrees Fahrenheit (F). The fiery burnup of fuel that sent *Apollo 8* soaring reached a maximum temperature of only 2500 degrees F—plenty hot but not even half the temperature the rocket had been engineered to withstand.

Still, when the question of what could go wrong was asked about the *Apollo 8* mission, the only reasonable answer had to be: *plenty*—and at every stage of the mind-bendingly complex mission.

At liftoff, if any one of the Saturn V's five engines failed to ignite properly, the rocket might stall and topple over before even clearing the launchpad. The three-stage booster, at that point a lit fuse attached to a colossal store of combustible liquid propellent, might simply explode on blastoff or in the moments just afterward.

At about eleven minutes into the flight, the CSM with the astronauts aboard, and the Saturn V third stage that was still attached to it, might fail to attain the velocity needed for slipping into Earth orbit. The third stage's engine was designed to achieve this critical acceleration in speed before shutting down, and it too had to work exactly as planned.

Next, when the time came for the astronauts to break free of their Earth orbit and head for the Moon, the third stage engine would have to refire at their command. To overcome Earth's gravitational pull, this maneuver required an increase in speed to "escape velocity." NASA had devised a typically geeky name for this phase of the journey: "Translunar Injection," or TLI. After powering the astronauts toward their destination, the third stage would detach from the CSM and the service module's own thruster rocket would perform the same function for later phases of the mission.

Then, as *Apollo 8* neared the Moon, another adjustment in speed, this time a slowdown, would be required to ease the CSM into lunar orbit—and prevent it from crashing headlong into the Moon's surface.

Twenty hours after that, when it was time to return to Earth, still another round of thruster bursts would be needed, once again to increase the CSM's velocity to the staggering 24,000-plus miles per hour that was optimal for the flight back home. If the thruster failed to fire at this stage, the module would remain in perpetual lunar orbit long after the astronauts had run out of oxygen, food, and water, as a weird kind of flying tomb and ghastly reminder to the world of the American space program's disastrously hasty attempt to make history.

Just as important as reaching the correct reentry velocity was

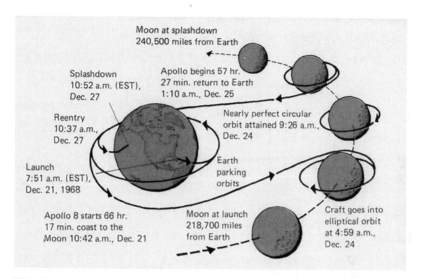

Moon at splashdown
240,500 miles from Earth

Splashdown
10:52 a.m. (EST),
Dec. 27

Apollo begins 57 hr.
27 min. return to Earth
1:10 a.m., Dec. 25

Reentry
10:37 a.m.,
Dec. 27

Nearly perfect circular
orbit attained 9:26 a.m.,
Dec. 24

Launch
7:51 a.m. (EST),
Dec. 21, 1968

Earth
parking
orbits

Apollo 8 starts 66 hr.
17 min. coast to the
Moon 10:42 a.m., Dec. 21

Moon at launch
218,700 miles
from Earth

Craft goes into
elliptical orbit
at 4:59 a.m.,
Dec. 24

This diagram shows key stages in the *Apollo 8* mission route and timeline.

the positioning of the space capsule at precisely the right angle of approach. Tilted just a few too many degrees one way, and the command module would skim off the edge of the Earth's atmosphere rather than penetrate it, and send the astronauts ricocheting into deep space, never to return home. A few too many degrees the other way, and the module would pierce the Earth's atmosphere unprotected by its heat shield and burn up instantly—long before the time for parachute deployment and splashdown. Bill Anders compared the level of accuracy required to position the module for reentry to "putting a letter in a letter slot in your door [from] twenty miles away."

During their rapid return to Earth, the astronauts would be barreling through space in a capsule cocooned within a fireball burning at temperatures approaching 5000 degrees F. At that stage, their fate depended on the capsule's heat shield functioning flawlessly. Even if it did, the parachutes designed to slow the module's final descent would also have to open fully and on schedule for the astronauts to make it safely back home. NASA employed a team of specially trained handlers whose sole job was to fold and pack the parachutes in just the right way to ensure that they would not become tangled on release.

When Susan Borman, who feared the worst for the fast-tracked mission, bluntly asked NASA flight director Chris Kraft about her husband's chances of survival, he replied without hesitation: "Fifty-fifty." The crew commander's wife knew Kraft well enough to tell he was leveling with her. Having prepared herself for even worse news, Susan Borman simply thanked Kraft and said: "Good, that suits me fine."

Bill Anders had made his own calculation, and it was not all that rosier. He gave the *Apollo 8* crew a one-third chance of total success; a one-third chance of surviving but without reaching the Moon; and a one-third chance of not coming back at all.

Ø

On September 14, the Soviet Union secretly launched the *Zond 5* spacecraft on a lunar trajectory. Three days later, as the space vehicle approached its destination, it looped once around the Moon and, rather than settling into an orbital pattern, continued as planned back to Earth, where it was recovered in the Indian Ocean. No cosmonauts—human or canine—had been sent on the mission, but Soviet scientists had stowed a curious assortment of smaller living creatures and organic material onboard for testing afterward for radiation exposure and other impacts of travel beyond the Earth's atmosphere. These included two Russian steppe tortoises and some worms, flies, and seeds. A mannequin wired with radiation sensors is said to have been strapped into the pilot's seat.

At first, Americans monitoring the flight had believed that *Zond 5* was the crewed Moon mission the US had feared; they thought this in part thanks to an elaborate prank the Soviets played on them. On September 19, a trio of cosmonauts hooked up a live transmission of their ground chatter in such a way as to make it *seem* to be coming from Zond. The cosmonauts were in

A Soviet postage stamp of 1969 heralded the triumph of *Zond 5*, the first spacecraft in history to circle the Moon.

fact speaking from the Soviet space program's command center in Yevpatoria, Crimea.

When the CIA intercepted the transmissions, they rose to the bait and immediately warned the White House that a Soviet Moon landing was imminent. On hearing this dire news, a furious President Johnson in turn called Frank Borman, demanding to know exactly what was going on. It is not clear how quickly NASA, the CIA, or the president realized they had been had. Borman later spoke, only half in jest, of the Soviet "hooligans" who had brought down a presidential earful on his head and caused him and others at NASA several heart-stopping moments.

Then on November 10, the Soviets launched *Zond 6*. The rapid follow-up to *Zond 5* may have been timed to further unnerve the Americans with its obvious echo of the *Sputnik* one-two punch. *Zond 6*, in any case, was more than enough to set off fresh NASA alarm bells.

In a dazzling show of technological prowess, the Soviets had launched the uncrewed probe from a satellite already in Earth orbit and had programmed it to fly by the Moon on an advanced data-gathering mission that included close-up photography of the lunar surface—presumably for the purpose of identifying a landing site. To NASA officials, the November probe had all the earmarks of a final dry run ahead of a crewed Moon mission. NASA also knew, however, that time for the Soviets was fast running out. Because a Moon shot would have to be timed to the relative positions of the Earth and Moon, and with other critical factors all in alignment, the Soviets' window for 1968 would close after December 10. As officials in Houston continued their preparations for *Apollo 8*, they counted down the days to the 10th and braced for the worst.

6

NO ORDINARY TIME

NASA's launch and splashdown dates, like those of the Soviets, were set with pinpoint precision based on a range of critical factors.* Once the new *Apollo 8* plan had been approved, the computers in Houston were fed all the relevant data and responded by presenting a two-day window for an end-of-year liftoff: December 20 and 21.

These dates, however, posed a special complication, as a launch on either day would put the astronauts in lunar orbit on Christmas Eve. What message, NASA officials felt obliged to ask, might people around the world—Christians *and* non-Christians—read into the coincidence? Would it be taken as a universal peace gesture or as a religious—or sacrilegious—one, or as something else altogether? And what if the mission went terribly wrong and the news of the deaths of three American astronauts cast a pall on the holiday season that could last for a generation or longer?

---

*In selecting a launch "window," or cluster of optimal dates for carrying out a space mission, NASA considered several factors. The location of the Earth in its orbit around the Sun was a key determinant, as was the projected location of the Moon or other target at the time the space vehicle would be reaching it. For safety's sake, NASA almost always timed its missions to allow for both a launch and recovery in broad daylight. An exception was made for the fast-tracked *Apollo 8*, whose scheduled Pacific splashdown was set for a good two hours before sunrise.

The *Apollo 8* crew (from left: Anders, Lovell, and Borman) are shown here in a training session at the Manned Spacecraft Center's Human Acceleration Facility in Houston. The spinning centrifuge into which they were strapped allowed the astronauts to experience extreme rates of acceleration and gravitational pressures that approximated the forces they would need to endure during their mission.

The year 1968 had already been one of the most violent years in American history since the Civil War.

In March, as the number of Vietnam War casualties continued to climb, growing opposition to the war had prompted President Johnson to announce his decision not to run for reelection. Johnson's expansion of the war had drained away much of the funding for his idealistic domestic agenda, which included a much-vaunted effort to end poverty in America.

In April, the civil rights leader Rev. Dr. Martin Luther King Jr. was assassinated while in Memphis to take part in a peaceful protest march of striking sanitation workers. Never

Protesters opposed to the Vietnam War marched in front of the White House on January 19, 1968. One sign expresses support for Eartha Kitt, the singer, actor, and activist who one day earlier had spoken out publicly against the war at a White House event attended by President Johnson.

an ardent supporter of NASA, King had questioned America's willingness to appropriate vast sums for the war in Vietnam and the space program, but not for efforts to fight poverty and end economic inequality in the world's richest democracy. In a speech the previous summer, he had said, "If our nation can spend $35 billion a year to fight an unjust, evil war in Vietnam and $20 billion to put a man on the Moon it can spend billion[s] of dollars to put God's children on their two feet right here on Earth." In response to King's murder, riots erupted in cities across America. Countless storefronts and entire city blocks went up in flames.

Two months later, Senator Robert F. Kennedy, the late

On the day after Dr. Martin Luther King Jr.'s assassination in Memphis, Tennessee, a large crowd gathered in New York's Central Park to mourn his loss. The question posed by the sign visible in this photograph—"Who's next?"—was brutally answered just two months later when Senator Robert F. Kennedy was murdered following a presidential campaign appearance in Los Angeles.

president's younger brother and himself then a candidate for president, was also assassinated.

And in late August, violence broke out in the streets of Chicago as the leaders of a bitterly divided Democratic Party gathered to choose their party's nominee for the November presidential election.

For many Americans, these and other disturbing Earth-bound events and crises had taken the shine off NASA's lofty aims and ambitions. Songwriter P. F. Sloan summed up the skeptics' view in the searing lyrics of "The Eve of Destruction," a protest ballad popularized by folk singer Barry McGuire: "Ah, you may leave

→ 12 → 12 A

Following the assassination of Dr. Martin Luther King Jr., in April 1968, riots broke out in cities across the United States, including the nation's capital where, during four days of violent protests, thirteen people were killed, about a thousand were injured, and numerous buildings were burned to the ground.

here for four days in space / But when you return, it's the same old place."*

The news media could no longer be counted on to treat the space program as an upbeat story that large numbers of Americans were eager to follow. At a pre-launch *Apollo 8* press conference at Houston Mission Control on December 7,

*Barry McGuire's recording of Sloan's impassioned anti-war song hit the coveted number one spot on the Billboard Hot 100 chart on September 25, 1965.

Police officers and members of the National Guard faced off—and clashed violently—with anti-Vietnam War protesters in the streets of Chicago as delegates to the Democratic National Convention met in late August 1968 to select the party's nominee for president.

journalists peppered the astronauts with questions about the timing of their mission, trying unsuccessfully to goad at least one of them into acknowledging that a journey to the Moon scheduled to occur on and about Christmas Eve could have been planned for no other reason than as a brazen publicity stunt.

One reporter also pointedly asked Bill Anders why a team of robots could not do the astronauts' jobs as well as they could, but at far less expense to taxpayers and without any risk to human life. The astronaut responded in his forthrightly folksy way that *Apollo 8* would mark humankind's first chance to have "an eyeball connected to a brain connected to an arm that can write or a tongue that can speak [about what the Moon was really like]. We think that by having a man in space, you can do a job that you can't do with unmanned vehicles."

Among the jobs Anders had to have been thinking about just then were his own duties as *Apollo 8*'s mission photographer. He had come to the assignment with no special experience with a camera, not even as a hobbyist. But he was determined to do his usual thorough job, and as mission planning proceeded, Anders researched the equipment he was to have with him. He concluded that to make the most of the superb Hasselblad EL camera NASA had chosen for the mission, he should also have a powerful (and heavy) 250-millimeter Zeiss Sonnar telephoto lens at his disposal.

SPACE CAMERA

The *Apollo 8* astronauts brought along two Hasselblad still cameras to record their mission.

Starting in 1962, NASA considered the Swedish-made 70-mm Hasselblad camera standard equipment for its crewed missions. Ruggedly built, easy to use, and motorized, it could take multiple exposures of a fast-changing scene. Film

came in "magazines" that were easily attached to the back
of the camera, allowing for quick reloading and switching
back and forth between black-and-white and color. The
optics company worked closely with mission planners
to peel precious ounces off the camera's overall weight,
increase the exposure count of its magazines, and to give
the camera's boxy housing a special matte black finish that
minimized reflections in the window of the spacecraft.
During the flight, magazines pre-loaded with film were
attached to the cabin walls with Velcro both to keep them
near at hand and to prevent them from floating about the
command module.

Every item considered for onboarding had to justify the space it would occupy and the weight it would add, and some at NASA thought the jumbo lens overkill. Anders, however, perhaps because he invariably had a solid reason for whatever he did, got his wish anyway. NASA's photo guru Richard W. Underwood taught him the basics of using the Hasselblad in space and lent him a NASA camera to practice on at home.

Following the press conference, the astronauts flew back to the Kennedy Space Center to quarantine in special quarters arranged to keep germs (and the media) at bay. There, with a private chef on call to help keep up their spirits, they were to rest, reflect, and continue reviewing their minute-by-minute flight plan.

Cut off from the world in this way, it was almost as if their journey to the Moon had already begun. Borman, in a somber mood, wrote a farewell letter to his family to be opened in the event he did not make it home alive. Anders recorded his last goodbyes to his wife and five children on an audio tape cassette.

Only Lovell chose not to worry about the future. Instead, he pored over NASA satellite photographs of the lunar surface, searching for a rock formation with a shape distinctive enough to use as a navigational landmark. Finally, he found one that fit the bill: a triangle-shaped mountain that he knew would be easy to spot. Lovell, the eternal romantic, scribbled a note that stated he wished to name his discovery "Mount Marilyn," in honor of his wife.

Then on December 8 came word from Houston that President and Mrs. Johnson had decided to host a White House state dinner in their honor—and that the gala event was to take place on the very next evening. The crew would be joined by their wives and twenty other members of the astronaut corps as well as by NASA flight director Chris Kraft; Wernher von Braun, the master architect of the Saturn V rocket; James E. Webb, the legendary former head of NASA; and the still more legendary aviator Charles Lindbergh and his wife, author Anne Morrow Lindbergh.

The star-studded event, tailor-made for worldwide press coverage, had been designed to tell a big story about America's contribution to aviation history—and, not least, the president's own role in it. Of course, the special dinner would also give

Borman and his crewmates a send-off to remember on behalf of a grateful nation.

Or would it? Johnson's timing could hardly have been worse. A deadly global flu pandemic was peaking just then, and with the astronauts' health a major concern, NASA doctors recommended against attending the gathering. The president had made up his mind, however, and would not be denied what was likely to be his last hurrah as he prepared to leave office in January—a once-mighty leader brought down by a stubborn commitment to a wrongheaded war. Every Apollo astronaut, he may have told himself, had a backup trained and ready to go, so what did it matter?

In any case, it was clear that the president did not have the *Apollo 8* astronauts' best interests foremost in mind as he posed and preened in the ballroom brimming with honored guests, some of whom, Bill Anders's wife, Valerie, could not help but notice with alarm, were coughing and sneezing all evening.*

Following the dinner, the astronauts returned to the Kennedy Space Center and resumed their quarantine. All three, as it turned out, seemed to have avoided the flu, and on December 15, at precisely 7:00 P.M. Eastern Standard Time, NASA began the official *Apollo 8* countdown at T minus 103 hours. With six days to liftoff, officials opted to bend the quarantine rules a bit

*Among the evening's highlights was Johnson's presentation of the Presidential Medal of Freedom to James E. Webb, the recently retired NASA chief administrator who had played a leading role in putting NASA on a realistic path to meeting President Kennedy's audacious goal, not least by successfully lobbying Congress for the vast sums of money the space program needed to stay on track.

US president Lyndon B. Johnson (at podium) is shown here speaking—and apparently telling a joke—during a state dinner at the White House on December 9, 1968, twelve days before the *Apollo 8* launch. Frank Borman (at the table in front of the podium), William Anders, James Lovell, and their wives were among the evening's honored guests.

and allow the astronauts an occasional visitor to break up the monotony.

Jim Lovell and his wife, Marilyn, were given some time together. Bill Anders, a devout Catholic, had a lengthy visit from his childhood priest, the sheer duration of which began to spook Borman as it wore on and on.

Then on the morning of December 20, the day before launch, the crew were told to expect two special guests for lunch: Charles and Anne Lindbergh wanted to continue the conversation they had begun with the astronauts at the White House over dinner. Borman would have rather done without the last-minute distraction but still managed to have a good time, chatting with the famous flier and sharing a laugh with him after Lindbergh asked how much fuel would be required for the astronauts' journey. On being told the huge quantity, Lindbergh jotted down some numbers on a slip of paper and replied that in one tenth of one second the Saturn V would burn an amount of fuel equal to that which he had carried onboard the *Spirit of St. Louis* for the whole of his thirty-three-and-a-half-hour solo flight across the Atlantic, in May 1927.

7

FIRE AND ICE

At last, December 21 arrived. At 2:36 A.M., Deke Slayton woke the astronauts and accompanied them for their preflight physical and traditional steak-and-eggs breakfast, where they were joined by Alan Shepard and a few other NASA veterans.

After that, it was time to suit up. Flight technicians hovering around each crew member attached sensors to the astronauts' bodies that would allow specialists on the ground to monitor their heart rate and other vital signs. They then helped Borman and the others climb into their cumbersome one-piece fire-resistant space suits, secured the astronauts' helmets and gloves, and hooked them up to their oxygen supply.

Apollo 8's Capcomm Michael Collins, the astronaut who later flew to the Moon as the third member of the *Apollo 11* crew, recalled that for him the first sensation of having left the Earth came not at liftoff, but in those last preflight hours when he and his crewmates were sealed inside their airtight suits. The sheer bulk of the protective all-white outfits, each more than twenty layers thick, made ordinary human activities like walking, stretching, and bending feel almost unnatural, and the suits'

From left, Frank Borman, Jim Lovell, and Bill Anders, all still in civilian clothes, sharing a light moment over the astronauts' traditional launch day breakfast of steak and eggs

built-in climate controls, which replaced the air they normally breathed with a steady flow of pure oxygen, effectively immersed them in a custom-made micro-environment that was not quite of this world. The suits also cut them off from most sensory stimuli. Apart from the amplified sound of their own breathing, Collins recalled: "You can hear only what is piped in over the radio; you can breathe only 100 percent oxygen, which is usually odorless; you can't feel much through the gloves. The only sense that is unimpaired is sight. You can see the world fine . . . [but] you really don't feel you are part of it."

As the astronauts trudged out the suiting-room door and boarded the van waiting to ferry them the three miles to the launch site, they looked for all the world like a trio of snowmen. Each astronaut carried an oxygen ventilator at his side that vaguely resembled a businessman's briefcase, and for a moment it seemed as though, except for their strange suits, Borman, Lovell, and Anders were just three more morning commuters heading off for another day at the office.

Bill Anders adjusts his snug-fitting "Snoopy cap"—nicknamed after the *Peanuts* comic strip character's aviator headgear. The astronauts' caps had built-in audio headsets.

Apollo 8 lifted off on schedule at 7:51 A.M. Eastern Standard Time. As the engines ignited, the Saturn V spat out great plumes of fire from below, boiled off massive clouds of hydrogen fuel, and shed a blizzard of ice shards from the coating of ice that had crystallized all up and down its length overnight. Unsuspecting onlookers might have assumed they were witnessing a major catastrophe.

For the astronauts themselves, the worst part of the initial ascent was the incredibly violent shaking of the three-stage rocket and everything attached to it, including themselves. The flight simulator had not come close to preparing them for this part of the journey—or for the earsplitting noise the engines

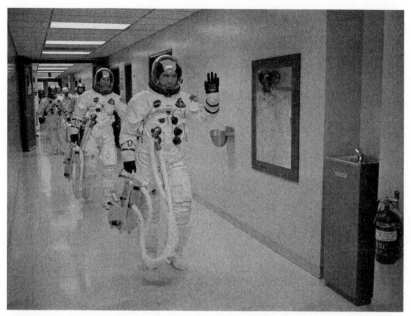

The crew, having donned their space suits and been wired with sensors, make their way to the minivan waiting to transport them to Launch Complex 39A.

generated, which NASA calculated to be the equivalent of ten thousand commercial jet engines firing simultaneously.

During liftoff, one of Borman's main tasks as commander was to keep one hand on an emergency "abort" handle for pulling in case the rocket was clearly in trouble.* Fearing, however, that the uncontrollable shaking of the rocket might cause him to pull the handle accidentally, Borman, who for a time could not hold himself steady enough to read the dials on his control panels, decided—with so much riding on the mission's success—to

*Doing so would instantly terminate the mission and catapult the CSM and crew up and away from the launchpad to safety.

The Saturn V launch vehicle lifting off as the *Apollo 8* mission finally gets underway

let go of the handle and simply hope for the best.

As all this was happening, Anders briefly convinced himself that the Saturn V must be on the verge of breaking apart; he later recalled feeling just then "like a rat being thrashed in the jaws of a terrier."

Spectators were permitted to take up positions within three and a half miles of the launch site. Those who did so recalled the ground shaking underfoot as if from a powerful earthquake. The accompanying sound, they said, could have been that of a huge explosion.

Anne Morrow Lindbergh, who witnessed the launch with her husband from the VIP viewing stand, put a poetic spin on the liftoff, writing afterward that it had appeared to unfold "slowly, as in a dream, so slowly [that the Saturn V rocket] seemed to hang suspended on the cloud of fire and smoke."

Susan Borman, who had stayed home and watched the launch on TV surrounded by family and friends, was apparently just as thrilled. Seeing the "awesome" Saturn V climb up into the sky, she said, was like "watching the Empire State Building taking off."

Ø

Frank Borman moving about inside the *Apollo 8* command module

The next three days on board *Apollo 8* were busy ones that left the crew with little time to reflect on what was happening to them.

Approximately eleven minutes into the flight, the astronauts, with the Saturn V's third stage still attached to the CSM, slipped into Earth orbit, and remained in a parking orbit for nearly the next three hours as the crew made a final check of the spacecraft's key systems and equipment.

Twenty-four minutes into the flight, as they continued to circle the planet, Lovell suggested that they take off their helmets and bulky gloves: "I mean, let's get comfortable," he said. "This is going to be a long trip." Four minutes later, Borman, understated as usual, made his first comment about the nerve-racking blastoff they had all just survived: "That was quite a ride, wasn't it?"

Achieving Earth-orbital insertion had been the first of several critical maneuvers on the astronauts' to-do list. Up next was the Translunar Injection burn, or TLI, designed to send the CSM coasting straight for the Moon. When the moment for this came at 10:42 A.M., or two hours and fifty minutes into the mission, Borman ignited the third-stage Saturn engine.*

The astronauts were flying over Hawaii just then, and spectators on the ground at Maui reported witnessing the engine's brief, fiery flash which, at that exact moment, caused the crew of *Apollo 8* to become the first humans ever to venture beyond the Earth's gravitational influence. Moments later, as *Apollo 8* continued to accelerate from about 17,400 to 24,226 miles per hour, the crew also became the fastest-moving humans in history.

But not everything went as planned. At one hour and thirteen minutes, Lovell's life vest accidentally inflated after catching on a tank fixed to the cabin wall. Minutes later, the mission navigator was also scrambling to find any space big enough to stow his fish-bowl helmet. The crew had been instructed *not* to look out the cabin windows lest the distraction result in some error in judgment. But at three hours and thirty-five minutes, Lovell took a peek anyway and reported excitedly to Mission Control: "We have a beautiful view of Florida now. We can see the Cape. . . . And at the same time, we can see Africa. West Africa is beautiful. I can also see Gibraltar at the same time I'm looking at Florida."

On day two of the mission—or Sunday afternoon at about

---

*After this maneuver, the third stage separated from the CSM, which had its own engine for use in making later adjustments to the astronauts' travel speed.

This photograph of the Moon was taken from the *Apollo 8* command module on December 22, 1968.

3:00 P.M. ET—*Apollo 8*, now more than halfway to the Moon, began beaming back the first of six scheduled live television broadcasts to viewers around the world.

When Anders switched on the camera, only two of the crew members were in a suitably lighthearted mood, however. Anders himself, the only astronaut onboard for whom weightlessness was a completely new experience, was eager to share the fun of life without gravity with folks on the ground. He gamely twirled his toothbrush in front of his nose before trying to capture it between his teeth. (After some technical difficulties, he also gave viewers a brief glimpse of Earth through one of the cabin windows, though the image was so fuzzy it made little or no impression.)

Lovell demonstrated the use of his sextant, showed viewers how to prepare chocolate pudding astronaut-style, and wished his seventy-three-year-old mother, Blanche, a happy birthday.

Borman, however, who hours earlier had exhibited worrisome flu-like symptoms, wanted only to be seen on camera manning the controls.* He had opposed taking along television equipment, arguing that the camera would add nothing to the mission besides excess weight.

The brief transmission, which in some time zones interrupted a CBS broadcast of an NFL playoff game between the Minnesota Vikings and Baltimore Colts—the ultimate league champions that season—prompted a flood of complaints from outraged fans.** Be that as it may, the astronauts still had five more live broadcasts on their mission checklist to get through; the fourth of these was scheduled not for any old time either, but Christmas Eve.

By the second broadcast, which came at hour fifty-five of the flight, Anders had solved the visibility problem and was able to treat viewers to a real-time black-and-white image of Earth— the first ever seen on television.

*Borman turned out not to have the flu and was feeling much better a day later.

**Borman himself initially sided with the fans but later changed his mind about the value of sharing the astronauts' inflight experience with the public via live television broadcasts from space.

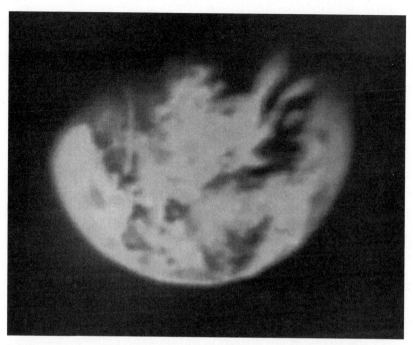

Earth dwellers were treated to this fuzzy, real-time view of the Earth's western hemisphere during the second live *Apollo 8* television broadcast, on December 23, 1968.

For this program, Lovell did most of the talking. First, he named several far-flung geographical features that he could see all at once from *Apollo 8*'s unique vantage point: the North Pole, Baja California, Gulf of Mexico, Cape Horn. Then, as if to prove he was not just making it all up, he remarked in detail on what he could tell about current weather conditions in various regions of the world. Finally, the audience heard from Lovell the dreamer: "What I keep imagining is, if I'm some lonely traveler from another planet, what [would I] think about the Earth at this altitude, [would I think] it's inhabited or not."

This photograph of the Mission Operations Control Room of the Mission Control Center in Houston was taken on December 23, 1968, or day 3 of *Apollo 8*. Visible on several of the screens is an image of Earth from the television broadcast.

Apollo 8 had come within fifty thousand miles of its destination at precisely fifty-five hours, thirty-eight minutes, and the crew made history again as they entered the Moon's gravitational field and thus became the first human explorers ever to be wholly subject to the natural forces of a celestial body other than Earth's.

At Mission Control in Houston, the technicians' display screens briefly flickered in unison as the running numerical tally of *Apollo 8*'s distance from Earth switched over to a tally of its distance from the lunar surface.

Toward the end of day three, *Apollo 8* traversed the front side of the Moon at a distance of about seventy miles—the closest by far that humans had ever come to it. Oddly, the astronauts could still not see the Moon for themselves, as the CSM's windows were turned away from it. Anders compared their view of "nothing" just then to that of a crew in a submerged submarine.

Before long, the astronauts had made their way around to the Moon's back or "dark side"—which isn't always shrouded in total darkness after all.*

The time was fast approaching for the maneuver that would ease the CSM into lunar orbit. This procedure—one of the most dangerous of the entire mission—required another carefully timed and measured burst from the service module's Service Propulsion System engine, or SPS. The goal was to slow the CSM just enough to allow it to be captured by the Moon's gravity, but not enough for it to be pulled crashing downward onto the lunar surface.

Even a slight miscalculation or equipment failure would likely result in catastrophe. Adding to the drama, the engine burn was to occur while the CSM was still on the dark side, when the Moon would be blocking all communication signals to and from Mission Control.

For nearly half an hour, no one on Earth would know if the crew had achieved lunar orbit—or perished trying. One minute and counting before LOS, or loss of signal, Houston informed the crew, "All systems Go," to which Lovell, ever the glass-half-full guy, blithely replied, "We'll see you on the other side."

---

*The same side of the Moon is always facing our planet, because the time it takes the Moon to complete one full orbit around Earth is equal to the time it takes the Moon to complete one full rotation on its own axis. However, the "dark" side of the Moon does receive some light from the Sun, even though we can't perceive it from Earth.

8

"LIVE FROM THE
MOON . . ."

When Houston's radio contact with *Apollo 8* started up again at the expected time, wild cheers erupted at Mission Control. The CSM had settled into a lunar parking orbit and begun the first of ten scheduled revolutions.

It was finally time then for all three astronauts to set aside whatever else they were doing and gaze out at the extra-

As *Apollo 8* orbited the Moon, Bill Anders recorded numerous close-up views like this one of the lunar landscape.

ordinary locale in which they found themselves.

The astronauts were still flying over the dark side, which at first was *too* dark for the crew to make out anything of the rugged, pock-marked terrain. It was not long, however, before, as Lovell recalled, "shards of sunlight started to illuminate the peaks of

This photographic study of the Moon's "dark" or far side was taken from the command module looking straight down. It depicts the rugged terrain of an approximately 400-square-mile patch of the lunar surface.

craters just sixty miles below. Finally the far side was bathed in sunlight and we stared in silence as the ancient far side craters slowly passed beneath. I was observing ... that part of the Moon that had been hidden from man for millions of years."

Anders's impressions of the strange scene unfolding before them were a lot more down-to-earth. The dark side, he later recalled, had reminded him of the "sandpile my kids have been playing in for some time. It's all beat up, no definition, just a lot of bumps and holes."

From then until the time came nearly two days later for the long journey home, the astronauts, Capcomm Michael Collins recalled, "chattered like excited tourists."

Anders's top priority as *Apollo 8*'s photographer was to capture detailed images of those portions of the lunar surface that looked most promising as landing sites for future missions. High-resolution photographs also offered mission scientists the chance to solve age-old mysteries about the Moon's geology, such as the physical makeup of its outermost layer. How rock-solid, or powdery, *was* the lunar surface? Just what would happen when the LM touched down on it? Would it kick up clouds of dust, perhaps enough particles to interfere with visibility or damage the LM?

A few scientists even believed the Moon might be blanketed by a coating of dust so thick—possibly as much as thirty or more feet deep in places—that, on landing, the LM would sink into the ground and get stuck there permanently. Most scientists did not think this scenario likely, but high-res, close-up photographs could likely answer that question and others once and for all.

While no one at NASA doubted photography's value as a precision tool for resolving technical issues like these, a major difference of opinion divided agency officials when it came to putting cameras to use for other purposes. Skeptics feared that if the astronauts spent precious time documenting their impressions of how it *felt* to venture far from Earth, critics might accuse NASA of frivolous space tourism—and urge Congress to cut off funding for the agency.

MISSING PHOTOS

The most unfortunate result of NASA officials downplaying the importance of photographic documentation came —incredibly—with the Apollo 11 *landing, when not even one still photograph of Neil Armstrong was taken during the nearly twenty-two hours he spent as the first human to set*

A reflection of Neil Armstrong, who took this photo of fellow Moon walker Edwin ("Buzz") Aldrin, is visible in Aldrin's visor.

foot on the Moon. No one at Mission Control had thought to add an image matching that description to the astronauts' checklist of high priority photographic targets. As a consequence, none was made. The only still images we have of Armstrong on the Moon are those later extracted from the video footage—plus the tiny reflection of Armstrong that can be glimpsed in Buzz Aldrin's visor in a photo Armstrong himself snapped of his crewmate.

Richard W. Underwood, the engineer in charge of NASA photography, disagreed strongly with the agency's official policy. He was convinced, in fact, that photos that gave ordinary people a clear sense of what the astronauts had seen and experienced were of the utmost importance and would likely be the thing NASA was best remembered by years later, long after the reams of technical images and scientific data that the astronauts harvested had become obsolete. He urged the astronauts to whom he gave photography lessons not to get fancy, but rather to bring back images that would give everyone the chance to see something of what they themselves had been privileged to see with their own eyes.

The *Apollo 8* mission plan that Borman and his crew had along with them classified the Earth as a low-priority photographic subject. Nonetheless, Underwood made certain that Anders and his crewmates understood the "earthrise" phenomenon—how the planet would appear to rise above the lunar horizon each time they orbited around from the far side of the Moon, provided their windows were facing in the right direction. With this training in mind, the crew would be prepared to capture it on film when the opportunity came their way.

On December 24, with *Apollo 8* in its fourth lunar orbit, Borman performed a scheduled maneuver to reorient the CSM. Until then, the astronauts had been circling the Moon seated backward and (by Earth standards) upside down. As they peered out the module's five small rectangular windows, the astronauts had an excellent view of the gritty, gray lunar terrain—but not of Earth.

Now, however, as Borman rotated the vehicle, the planet swung into view as a breathtakingly beautiful sight. Anders had been chatting animatedly with Mission Control about some lunar impact crater that had caught his attention when Borman suddenly broke in with a rush of excitement that neither Anders nor Lovell had ever heard in his voice before.

"Oh, my God," Borman called out. "Look at that picture over there. There's the Earth coming up. Wow, is that pretty!"

Later accounts of the moment made it sound as if Borman had been taken by surprise by the sight of the shimmering blue and white Earth-ball floating in space. But thanks to Richard Underwood, this of course had not been the case.

To know something out of the ordinary *may* happen, however, is not the same thing as experiencing it for yourself when it does, and for once, Frank Borman, the austere, buttoned-down test pilot, engineering geek, and Cold Warrior par excellence found himself utterly overcome with amazement.

As Borman reached for the spare Hasselblad, Anders could not help ribbing his by-the-book commander for having just gone wildly off script: "Hey, don't take that," he mock scolded him. "It's not scheduled."

As all three astronauts chortled at the joke, Borman clicked away. The black-and-white photos he took then came to be thought of afterward as the dress rehearsal for the *Earthrise* photograph Anders was moments away from recording for posterity.

As mission photographer, Anders now decided that Borman's

black-and-white photos would not suffice and, with his own Hasselblad already in hand, he called out to Lovell to pass him a magazine with color film—quick.

"Got it?" Lovell muttered, sounding agitated as he handed over the film. A moment later, the usually easygoing navigator was barking orders at Anders: "Take several [photographs], take several of 'em." Then, still not satisfied, Lovell demanded: "Here, give it [the camera] to me."

This image of what Anders actually saw in his viewfinder was later rotated ninety degrees to make it more readily understandable for earthlings accustomed to viewing the Sun and Moon rise and set in up-and-down movements.

Lovell's competitive instincts had been aroused.

But Anders, the seasoned fighter pilot, held on to the Hasselblad: "Wait a minute," he told Lovell in a calming voice, "let's get the right setting." And then, reminding the mission navigator to let him do his job, Anders added: "Just calm down."

At this point commander Borman chimed in with an end-of-discussion "Calm down, Lovell!"

Life inside *Apollo 8* returned to normal, and Anders confirmed that he had indeed captured the photograph they all knew was going to be special. He was absolutely sure of it, Anders said.

The next few hours were taken up with snapping more

pictures of the lunar surface and with the exhausted Lovell and Anders taking their planned sleep breaks. Borman, who had napped earlier, monitored the controls while his colleagues rested. At one point he reported to Collins in Houston, "Lovell's snoring already." The Capcomm answered, "Yes, we can hear him down here."

More excitement awaited the crew later that day. At about 8:30 P.M. Houston time, Anders once again switched on the onboard television camera. Frank Borman, who by then had warmed up to the role of TV host, introduced the astronauts' Christmas Eve special with a matter-of-fact: "This is *Apollo 8* coming to you live from the Moon."

No one at NASA had bothered to prepare a script for the astronauts; the agency's media consultant simply told the three men to say "whatever's appropriate."

The crew had decided among themselves to start by recounting their first impressions of seeing the Moon at close range, followed by a brief reading of the opening lines of Genesis, the Old Testament's creation story.*

As the broadcast began, the CSM's windows were fogged over, making it impossible at first for Anders to give viewers

---

*The crew had used some of their time holed up in pre-flight quarantine to plan their Christmas Eve television broadcast, which was sure to be viewed by a vast global audience. Borman asked a publicist friend, Simon Bourgin, for ideas, and Bourgin asked journalist Joe Laitin who, in turn, asked his wife. Christine Laitin responded by suggesting, "Why don't you begin at the beginning?" and pointed to the opening verses of Genesis as the ideal text for an occasion when people everywhere were being invited to see the Earth, the Moon, and the universe itself in a new way. Before the actual broadcast, the astronauts waited almost until the last minute to decide who would read which of the pre-selected verses from Genesis.

another glimpse of the Earth from which—surreally—they themselves were watching. But as usual Anders soon had everything up and running and got the show off to a good start with sharp on-camera images of both the Earth *and* the Moon.

Borman spoke first: "The Moon is a different thing to each one of us . . . I know my own impression is that it's a vast, lonely, forbidding-type existence or expanse of nothing; it looks rather like clouds and clouds of pumice stone . . . And it certainly would not appear to be a very inviting . . . place to live or work."

Next it was Lovell's turn: "My thoughts were very similar," he said. "The vast loneliness . . . of the Moon is awe-inspiring, and it makes you realize what you have back there on Earth. The Earth from here is a grand oasis in the big vastness of space."

Then Anders added: "I think the thing that impressed me the most was the lunar sunrises and sunsets. These, in particular, bring out the stark nature of the terrain, and the long shadows really bring out the relief that is here and hard to see in this very bright surface that we're going over right now."

Next Anders trained the video camera on the lunar surface and for the next several minutes the crew gave viewers a real-time guided tour of the strange craters and lunar landforms that flickered across their screens. An estimated one billion viewers in sixty-four countries—or nearly one in three of all living humans—had tuned in to the broadcast, making it the most widely viewed television show in history. Perhaps it

And God made the firmament,

On Christmas Eve 1968, as the *Apollo 8* crew took turns reading the first verses of the creation story from the book of Genesis, millions of television viewers around the world were treated to close-up images of the Moon in real time, as seen in this captioned still from a video of the broadcast.

would hardly have mattered what the astronauts said. Still, it was Christmas Eve, at least for viewers in the Western hemisphere who observed the holiday, and as the astronauts sailed into view of a lunar sunrise that Anders was able to share on-screen, the moment seemed right to turn to the reading.

Anders made the graceful segue: "For all the people back on Earth, the crew of *Apollo 8* has a message that we would like to send to you." He then read the first four verses of Genesis, starting with "In the beginning God created the heaven and the earth . . ." Then Lovell read verses 5–8, and Borman concluded with Genesis 9–10: "And God said, 'Let the waters under the heaven be gathered together unto one place and let the dry land appear.' And it was so. And God called the dry land Earth, and the gathering together of the waters called these Seas. And God saw that it was good."

Twenty-six minutes after the start of the historic broadcast, a seemingly relaxed and satisfied Borman signed off with well wishes for everyone in the astronauts' vast, far-away audience: "And from the crew of *Apollo 8*, we close with good night, good luck, merry Christmas, and God bless all of you—all of you on the good Earth."

Even the once-skeptical mission commander had given his all in what turned out to be an unforgettable performance. Years later, he would say he had been wrong to oppose bringing a television camera along on the mission. He had changed his mind, he said, not for sentimental or spiritual reasons but for purely common-sense ones.

"Americans," Borman had decided, "deserved to see what they'd paid for."

9

THE WHOLE EARTH

After the camera was switched off, the conversation with Mission Control immediately turned to preparations for TEI, or Trans Earth Injection—*Apollo 8*'s reentry into the Earth's atmosphere.

The astronauts had already begun tidying up the cabin in preparation for the return trip, knowing that the powerful engine burn required to free them from lunar orbit would shake loose anything in the cabin that was not secured. "Store all the cameras," Borman had instructed the crew, "store everything because this burn will be a bang . . . Get the whole damn thing in ship-shape. Because now she's going to take us home!"

About three hours after the broadcast and following another check of the CSM's onboard equipment and systems, the crew executed TEI. Once again, *Apollo 8* was on the Moon's dark side during a critical maneuver and once again, officials in Houston—and the astronauts' families—all held their breath as they awaited news of the crew's fate.

Half a world away from Mission Control, an Australian tracking station picked up a signal from the spacecraft at precisely the expected time. NASA headquarters was unable to do so for another four tense minutes. The delay, it turned out, had nothing to do with an onboard problem; a very busy Bill Anders had simply forgotten to switch the right radio antenna back on.

When Anders finally did so, Lovell's buoyant voice was first to break the silence. His message to Mission Control, his family, and anyone else who might be listening was: "Please be informed—there is a Santa Claus." The engine had performed perfectly, positioning the CSM to within two-thousands of a degree of the optimal angle for reentry, a slight deviation that was well within the acceptable margin of error.

It was Christmas morning in Houston as the astronauts started their two-and-a-half-day journey back home, flying at speeds as high as 24,969 miles per hour.

The return flight did not start out as the uneventful homeward glide the astronauts might have wished for, however. Within a few hours of TEI, Lovell, still seriously short of sleep, punched the wrong code into the onboard computer, freezing the navigation system and throwing the command module off course. It took all three crew members working furiously for half an hour or more to prevent the capsule from spinning completely out of control and to restore it to its proper position for reentry. After that one terrifying incident, the rest of the flight went more or less as planned.

As it was still Christmas Day on the ground in Houston, the astronauts even took time out to share a holiday meal of dehydrated cranberry-apple sauce and turkey and gravy stowed in thermostabilized wetpacks brought along for the occasion.

On the morning of December 27, as *Apollo 8* plunged the last seventy-five miles back to Earth, the capsule's heat shield was finally put to the test. It performed well, protecting the vehicle from the fiery vapors that had enveloped its exterior walls, even as a few fist-sized chunks of the shield broke off and flew past the window where first-timer Bill Anders watched in horror, wondering darkly whether NASA had saved the very worst fright for last. Never at a loss for a vivid metaphor, he later recalled having felt just then "like a fly inside the flame of a blowtorch."

Once *Apollo 8* re-entered the Earth's atmosphere at an altitude of approximately 400,000 feet, the effective functioning of the command module's heat shield became a life-and-death matter. A tracking system camera attached to an Air Force refueling plane flying at 40,000 feet captured the fiery scene in the early hours of December 27.

Apollo 8 splashed down in the north Pacific at 9:51 A.M. Houston time, one thousand miles south-southwest of Hawaii. The crew had made a bull's-eye landing, touching down within three miles of where the recovery ship, the aircraft carrier USS *Yorktown*, had positioned itself.

The capsule, however, hit the water with a thud at an unexpected angle that caused it to flip over, sending loose garbage raining down on the astronauts. Because it was still nighttime in the recovery zone, the crew had to wait, strapped upside down in their

US Navy frogmen are shown here making preparations for transporting the *Apollo 8* command module and crew to the USS *Yorktown* following splashdown.

couches, for about two hours before they could be retrieved by helicopter and brought aboard the *Yorktown* for their heroes' welcome.

Having touched down in rough seas, the capsule rocked violently during all that long wait. After a while, Borman's stomach had had enough and the mission's no-nonsense commander vomited all over himself and his crewmates.

The live television coverage of *Apollo 8*'s triumphant return marked the start of the three astronauts' new lives as legendary space pioneers—and recipients of a seemingly endless stream of awards and accolades, not just from America's leaders but also from world heads of state, the Pope, and even the Soviet Union's usually hostile top officials.

People everywhere seemed excited to celebrate the three men's achievement as not just an American triumph but a human one. For the crew, a medical checkup, a shower, and presidential telephone call were in the immediate offing, followed by their return to Houston, reunion with their families, and weeks and weeks of parades, speeches, banquets, and ceremonies.

To clear his head after this incredible rush of public attention, Frank Borman volunteered to work at a friend's Texas service station and briefly lost himself in the down-to-earth tasks of pumping gas for customers and repairing cars alongside the commander's two sons, all the while hoping not to be recognized by anybody.

Ø

After navy divers and pilots recovered the *Apollo 8* capsule and deposited it on the deck of the *Yorktown*, its precious cargo of film with nearly 1,100 still exposures were packed up and flown to Houston, where NASA's Richard Underwood had the photographs developed and printed immediately and with great care.*

Anders had not taken just one *Earthrise* photo but several. The agency, grasping the image's significance, chose what it considered the best version and on December 30 released it to the media.

*The *Apollo 8* astronauts also brought back 700 feet of 16-mm movie film, which for years remained in a vault along with other unseen NASA film footage until film director Al Reinert learned of the archive and was granted the use of it for his 1989 feature-length documentary *For All Mankind*.

A crowd of more than 2,000 people welcomed the returning *Apollo 8* crew at Ellington Air Force Base in Houston, Texas. Inset shows a close-up of astronauts (from left to right) Bill Anders, Frank Borman, and Jim Lovell standing side by side at the center of the jubilant crowd.

The *Earthrise* image NASA made public had been altered in two ways. It was cropped to make the Earth look larger within the picture frame than it had appeared to Anders; and it was rotated ninety degrees so that the Earth appeared to be rising up from below the lunar horizon rather than coming out of the Moon's side, which is how it had actually looked from the orbiting astronauts' vantage point.

Within hours, *Earthrise* appeared on the front pages of newspapers everywhere and instantly became one of the most widely seen photographs in history. Most newspapers at the time printed photographs only in black and white, but a few days later the glossy, full-color newsweeklies had their turn too and published *Earthrise* as it was meant to be seen. *Life* gave the photo a two-page color spread in its first issue for the new year just days after its sister publication, *Time,* featured the crew of *Apollo 8* on its cover as the influential newsweekly's 1968 "Men of the Year."

One reason the photograph made such a powerful impression is that it had been shot outside the Earth's atmosphere, in dust-free, atmosphere-less space, where there were no floating particles to refract light and cause even a slight blurring of the image. As a result, *Earthrise* had an extraordinary sharpness of focus that people were unaccustomed to in a photograph. Even apart from its unique subject matter, its impact was like that of a spectacular Hollywood "special effect."

Soon Anders's photograph was being put to other uses as well. During his last days in the White House, President Johnson handed out dozens of framed prints of *Earthrise* as parting

The *Earthrise* photo illustrated a year-in-review article on the front page of the December 31, 1968, issue of the *Beatrice Daily Sun*. This southeastern Nebraska daily was one of countless newspapers around the world to feature the NASA photograph on this day, along with a photo of the Moon's surface.

gifts to world dignitaries. In April 1969, the US Postal Service issued an *Earthrise* commemorative stamp.

That same spring, the image appeared in black and white

on the cover of a quirky, over-sized, environmentally minded magazine from San Francisco called *Whole Earth Catalog*. Both *Earthrise* and the popular catalog, which presented readers with a fascinating grab bag of useful information for those wishing to adopt an eco-friendly lifestyle, helped to inspire the first Earth Day celebration, which took place on April 22, 1970, and was observed in thousands of communities by an estimated twenty million Americans.

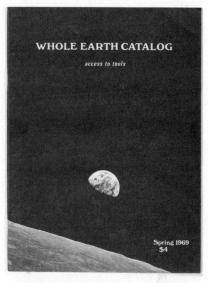

Earthrise appeared on the cover of *Whole Earth Catalog* in spring 1969.

Anders's photograph gave millions of non-scientists their first photographically accurate glimpse of the Earth as an object that was small, fragile, beautiful, and floating alone in an otherwise airless and infinite universe. It became the symbol not only of Earth Day but of the environmental movement that was rapidly gaining momentum in the US and around the world.

The clever young man responsible for producing *Whole Earth Catalog* was no ordinary *Earthrise* fan. Stewart Brand was a kind of professional daydreamer. He had studied biology, served in the army, and worked briefly as a photographer and rock-music concert promoter. A central figure of San Francisco's hippie movement—America's youthful, war-protesting, establishment-

offending countercul-
ture scene—Brand was
also an environmental-
ist, a performance artist,
an entrepreneur, and a
super salesman.

Some of Brand's
favorite daydreams were
those he had about the
future of the world.
Brand had not only
imagined a photograph

**THE WHOLE
EARTH IS WATCHING**

of the "whole earth" well
before Anders took the
one that NASA made
famous; in February

In this powerful Earth Day poster, the *Earthrise* image is reimagined as a watchful eye symbolizing humanity's concern for the future of the planet. The creator and year of this poster are unknown.

1966, he launched a one-man publicity campaign to persuade the US space agency to bring back such an image as a gift to the people of the world.

Brand's prankish lobbying effort began on a lazy, sun-splashed San Francisco afternoon when, as he gazed out from his rooftop at the shimmering skyline spread before him, he had what he was sure was a good idea. Brand had been reading a book by one of his heroes—Buckminster Fuller—an American architect and inventor with a special knack of his own for imagining the future. Fuller urged his readers to take responsibility for the well-being of their planet and to be less wasteful in their daily lives.

Brand's rooftop perch gave him an enviable view of the Bay Area, one of America's most beautiful urban settings. But the view Brand *really* wanted just then was one, like Fuller's, with a much wider perspective. As he pictured himself peering down at the Earth from a point somewhere far out in space, a catchy slogan started to form in his mind. It was a provocative slogan, he thought, that could be printed on buttons for like-minded folk to wear on their T-shirts and lapels as a way of spreading the word about the need to pay more attention to the planet as a whole.

Buckminster Fuller was a visionary American architect, inventor, and futurist who, through his copious and often colorful writings and experimental designs, played a pivotal role in shaping contemporary thought about the changing relationship of the built environment to the Earth—a planet, he argued, that could continue to support life only if its resources were properly safeguarded.

He decided that version one of his slogan—"Take a photograph of the entire Earth"—sounded too much like a demand. After some tinkering, he recast it as a question designed to pique people's curiosity. Brand ordered a good supply of buttons that asked people to wonder: "Why haven't we seen a photograph of the whole Earth yet?"

When the buttons were ready, Brand donned a white jumpsuit and showman's top hat and headed across the Bay Bridge to UC Berkeley, where he took up a position at the campus crossroads known as Sather Gate. With an old-fashioned salesman's sandwich board painted in Day-Glo lettering hanging from his shoulders, he began to parade back and forth to attract attention. Brand himself was a picture waiting to be taken! Soon people were stopping to chat and to purchase one of his buttons for a quarter. Campus security guards eventually noticed the visitor too, and told him to leave.

Stewart Brand personally sold the buttons he created for a quarter on college campuses and mailed buttons to NASA officials and government leaders as part of a one-man publicity campaign to promote environmental awareness.

As Brand took his one-man show on the road to other college campuses, stories about his campaign began to appear in newspapers around the country. Meanwhile, he also mailed buttons to NASA officials and their secretaries (who, he guessed, were more likely to wear the buttons than their bosses), and to members of Congress, UN dignitaries, and even high-ranking Soviet scientists and leaders.

Years later, Brand would meet a man who introduced himself as a retired NASA security officer. It had once been his job, the man said, to investigate the California hippie with buttons to sell. He and Brand shared a good laugh over this. The investigator had concluded that the young demonstrator's activities posed no threat to the space agency—and that in fact he, Brand, had made a valid point.

The security officer had gone so far as to close his report with a mild dig at his NASA superiors: "By the way, why *haven't* we seen a photograph of the whole Earth yet?"

10

NO PLACE LIKE HOME

Stewart Brand, it turned out, was not the first person to understand the potential power of a photo like *Earthrise*. British astron-
omer Fred Hoyle had done so nearly twenty years earlier. Hoyle
was so horrified by the violence of the Second World War that he
had felt compelled to think of a way to prevent another such war
from ever happening.

In his 1950 book, *The Nature of the Universe*, Hoyle suggested
that the key to securing peace was for humans everywhere to
reimagine their relationship to one another: to begin to see themselves not as citizens of this or that nation but rather as fellow
inhabitants of the same planet. Hoyle himself was hardly the first
person to champion the dream of a world without borders. But he
took the further step of proposing that the right photograph—like
a piece of persuasive evidence in a trial at court—might just possibly play a decisive role. He wrote that once the peoples of the
world had had the chance to actually see

> *a photograph of the Earth, taken from outside . . . we
> shall, in an emotional sense, acquire an additional*

Frank Borman's black-and-white photograph of Earth rising above the lunar surface, taken moments before Anders's famous color photograph

dimension . . . Let the sheer isolation of the Earth become plain to every man whatever his nationality or creed, and a new idea as powerful as any in history will be let loose[:] . . . the futility of national strife.

In the same year, an American science-fiction film, *Destination Moon*, gave moviegoers a glimpse of what a photograph like the one Hoyle envisioned would look like. In the movie's final scene, as the first four space travelers to set foot on the Moon are preparing their rocket ship for the journey home, a dramatic view of the whole Earth appears just over their shoulders and on the Moon's horizon. The artist who painted the backdrop had done a remarkably good job of imagining Earthrise. Even so, it was still only a Hollywood scenic painter's invention, and as such still just a kind of fantasy.

Hoyle and later Brand believed that a photograph—as an image plucked not from imagination but reality itself—might indeed have the power to change people's minds.

During the 1960s, Brand's role model, Buckminster Fuller, and one or two other future forecast-

A stamp commemorating *Earthrise* was issued by the US Postal Service on May 5, 1969. It includes a quote from the first line of Genesis echoing the biblical reading performed by the crew during their Christmas Eve telecast from space.

ers popularized a new metaphor for thinking about the planet that was, in effect, a new way of picturing it too. In their writings, they took to referring to the planet as "spaceship Earth." To some people, this seemed like a novel, fun way to imagine the planet: as not just the ground underfoot but also—from a larger perspective—as a kind of spacecraft whizzing through the cosmos with all humanity onboard. No need to don one of those cumbersome space suits after all! We humans were already rocketing through the universe!

SPACESHIP EARTH

British journalist and economist Barbara Ward may have coined the term in 1966 for her book Spaceship Earth, *in which she argued for the need to plan for the sustainability of life in an increasingly populous world with dwindling resources. That same year, economist Kenneth E. Boulding published an influential essay titled "The Economics of the Coming Spaceship Earth." But it was Buckminster Fuller who did the most to popularize the new view of a planet in peril.*

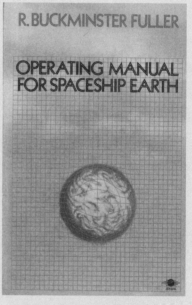

Fuller had been lecturing about "spaceship Earth" long before he published this widely read book of 1969. He may or may not have coined the title phrase, but with his extraordinary knack for holding an audience and making abstract concepts seem crystal clear, he certainly did more than anyone to popularize the phrase and the idea behind it.

Writing in 1969 in *Operating Manual for Planet Earth*, Fuller observed that if humans did not do more to safeguard the planet, they might one day have to rename their ruined paradise "Poluto."

At the same time, the image of the Earth as a spaceship served to highlight some of modern-day humankind's most serious concerns. By the 1960s, the combined threats of nuclear war and environmental catastrophe had made a great many people acutely aware of the Earth's fragility and its humbling smallness in the grand scheme of the universe. Like *Earthrise*, the phrase "spaceship Earth" was a vivid reminder that the planet, like any car or bicycle or spacecraft—or for that matter any living organism—needed to be cared for and not stretched past its limits.

Environmentalists embraced the idea of spaceship Earth and soon some high government leaders did so as well. In a stirring speech delivered at the United Nations, US Ambassador Adlai Stevenson urged his fellow delegates to take a moment to imagine themselves not as citizens of any one member nation but rather as fellow "passengers on a little spaceship, dependent on its vulnerable reserves of air and soil; all committed for our safety to its security and peace; preserved from annihilation only by the care, the work, and, I will say, the love we give our fragile craft."

In his conversations as Capcomm with the *Apollo 8* astronauts, Michael Collins thought he detected a change of perspective in all three crew members as they spoke about the home planet from which they had ventured so far: "I got the feeling from listening to them talk on the radio for a week," Collins said, "that they would always appreciate the Earth more because of their flight so far away from it."

Bill Anders summed up the change by saying: "We came all this way to explore the Moon, and the most important thing is that we discovered the Earth."

Less than seven months after *Apollo 8*'s return, the crew of *Apollo 11* finally met the challenge President Kennedy had set for the nation by landing two American astronauts on the surface of the Moon and returning them safely to Earth.

By the time the Apollo program came to an end with the splashdown of *Apollo 17* in December 1972, a total of twelve US astronauts—and none of any other nationality—had walked on the Moon. The crewed space program continued but as a series of orbital missions carried out first on NASA's Skylab Space Station (1973–1979), and then the NASA space shuttle (1981–2011), whose crews took part in the construction of the International Space Station that remains operational.

After Apollo, however, NASA shelved all efforts to send human explorers into deep space in favor of robotic probes like the Pathfinder mission to Mars, which deployed a small rover called *Sojourner* on the Martian surface in 1997.

No one could deny that sending astronauts to the Moon and back had been an extraordinary technological achievement. But what had it meant in *human* terms? Michael Collins became a thoughtful chronicler and interpreter of his space travels, but most

NASA astronauts proved to be better with high-tech electronics than they were with words. This was not entirely surprising, of course. Collins himself joked that while it might have been far more illuminating to send a poet, a philosopher, and a priest to the Moon, the odds of any of them making it back alive would have been much lower than those for the hardened test pilots NASA typically recruited for the job.

After the *Apollo 17* splashdown, a U.S. Navy helicopter positions itself to retrieve crew members for the short flight to the waiting aircraft carrier USS *Ticonderoga*, here seen in the distance.

In 1987, American science writer and self-styled "space philosopher" Frank White coined the term "overview effect" to describe a wide range of life-altering changes of mind and belief that Collins, *Apollo 17* commander Gene Cernan, and others who had viewed the Earth from deep space reported experiencing at the time or in later years.

Like Collins, Cernan was among the astronaut corps' more reflective members. Looking back at the Gemini and Apollo missions he had flown, he observed: "Being in Earth orbit vs going out beyond must be separated . . . Philosophically, we really have had two different space programs." Cernan added: "When you are in Earth orbit, you . . . are still part of the Earth—a system you can understand and relate to. When you leave Earth orbit . . .

you see a multicolored three-dimensional picture of Earth. You begin to see how little we understand of time. You ask yourself the question, 'Where really am I in space and time?' . . . and you say to yourself . . . if you could get everyone in the world up there, wouldn't they have a different feeling—a new perspective?"

Collins agreed with Cernan and went on to suggest an important contribution that new perspective might one day make toward improving life on Earth: "I really believe that if the political leaders of the world could see their planet from a distance of . . . 100,000 miles, their outlook would be fundamentally changed . . . [This] could be invaluable in getting people together to work out joint solutions, by causing them to realize that the planet we share unites us in a way far more basic and far more important than differences of skin color or religion or economic system. The pity of it is that so far the view from 100,000 miles has been the exclusive property of a handful of test pilots, rather than the world leaders who need this new perspective, or the poets who might communicate it to them."

Collins did not think his idea would be put into practice anytime soon, or that even a sharp increase in the number of crewed space flights would, by itself, ever bring about world peace. But he did believe that continued space exploration, and the humbling insights humans gleaned from it about their place in the universe, could make *some* difference over time.

Strikingly, the astronaut who may have done the most to realize a version of Collins's idea of space travel leading to world understanding was Cold Warrior Frank Borman, who in 1969 helped arrange the first joint US/Soviet space collaboration, the Apollo-Soyuz Project, which brought together orbiting crewed space vehicles from the two, longtime rival nations for an experimental docking maneuver.

Even so, when asked whether going to the Moon had altered his own core beliefs, Borman was dismissive. He told an interviewer: "Looking back at the Earth [from the Moon] was inspiring. But, you know, you go to the Grand Canyon and look around [and feel inspired there, too] . . . I find beauty [by]

In July 1975, less than three years after Project Apollo's final Moon landing, the US and Soviet Union joined forces for the crewed rendezvous and joint docking mission depicted here in an artist's rendering. The Apollo-Soyuz Test Project marked the start of a new era of international space research and exploration.

looking out here in this ... barren desert [in Las Cruces, New Mexico]! I think you either have an innate belief in a Spiritual Being or a God or you don't have. You don't have to go to the Moon ..." After *Apollo 8*, Borman had no interest in returning to space on another mission.

Collins seems to have shared Bill Anders's belief that the greatest benefit to him personally of having gone to the Moon was the deeper understanding it gave him for why the Earth should not be taken for granted. "Seeing the Moon up close," he wrote, "is really startling. When you are 60 miles away, you realize we are really lucky to be living on Earth. You ... have to see the 'second planet' [the Moon] to appreciate the first [the Earth]."

But James Lovell had quite a different reaction to his first lunar close encounter. As *Apollo 8* approached its destination, Lovell's initial sensation had been sheer delight at the realization that the Moon was "not too far from the Earth." For him, the experience had been one of wonder, not alienation. As he gazed out at the Moon from less than a hundred miles away, he had felt like a "schoolkid ... looking into a candy store window." It was as if he had stepped out his front door and gone for a walk without ever leaving his neighborhood. Lovell was not the only astronaut for whom the overview effect took the form of the thought, new to him, that the Earth and the Moon were not so much two separate places as two parts of the *same* place: the same human home.

Of the three *Apollo 8* astronauts, Bill Anders seems to have experienced the overview effect most intensely. Anders had grown up a devout Roman Catholic and had held fast to his faith throughout his years as a fighter pilot and astronaut. But as he later told a reporter, the sight of the distant Earth as a small and beautiful but also obviously insignificant object floating in the vastness of space "really undercut my religious beliefs. The idea that things rotate around the pope

Bill Anders on a visit to the San Diego Air & Space Museum in 1999.

and [that] up there is a big supercomputer wondering whether Billy was a good boy yesterday? It doesn't make any sense."

After *Apollo 8*, Anders turned away from traditional religion and refocused his energies on earthbound concerns, with the safeguarding of the environment high on his list.

Lovell and Anders teamed up again as fellow members of the backup crew for *Apollo 11*. But Frank Borman did not join them. Borman by then had taken a desk job as NASA's White House adviser. Soon afterward, Anders too accepted a high-level government position in Washington.

Only Lovell returned to space, in April 1970 as commander of *Apollo 13*, the lunar mission that narrowly escaped disaster when an oxygen tank in the Service Module exploded inflight, causing a rapid loss of precious oxygen and a breakdown of the electrical system. Lovell's prior experience with trial-by-fire emergency repair work during *Apollo 8* had helped prepare him to avert catastrophe a second time in this hair-raising mission, which people around the world closely followed in real time, almost as though it were a Hollywood thriller.* He retired from NASA in 1973 and afterward worked as an executive in various private businesses.

By the time NASA flew its final Moon mission, *Apollo 17*, in December 1972, public enthusiasm for the space program had waned considerably and Congress had begun to slash NASA's budget. Agency officials struggled in vain to define a new goal for the space program to rally around that had anything like the glamorous appeal and laser-like focus of President Kennedy's daring challenge.

Space stations orbiting the Earth, and space shuttles built to transport astronauts and supplies to those stations and back competed for scarce dollars with uncrewed missions to distant destinations like Mars and Saturn that at least had well-defined scientific research objectives and did not appear to the public—literally—to be going around and around in circles.

By *Apollo 17*, Moon landings had become so routine that many people did not bother to watch the live broadcasts on television. Scientists, however, applauded NASA for having included in that final mission's crew the first geologist assigned to study the Moon's surface. Like *Apollo 8*, the mission also was notable for a special photograph the astronauts brought back, the one that by Earth Day of the following year had come to be known around the world as the *Blue Marble*.

---

*A Hollywood thriller is exactly what it became. The film *Apollo 13* was released in 1995 with Tom Hanks in the starring role as Commander Jim Lovell.

Decades passed before NASA again made plans for crewed missions to the Moon and beyond. In 2017, the agency announced Artemis, a new space program whose goals included not only the return of astronauts to the Moon's surface but also the establishment of an international space station orbiting the Moon, construction of a base camp on the Moon itself, and the development of the advanced technologies needed to send a crewed mission to Mars.

In recent years, the space agencies of a handful of other nations have also achieved some success in the realm of lunar exploration. China landed *Chang'e-3*, the first of a series of uncrewed lunar probes, in 2013 with the clear intention of eventually sending humans to the Moon as well. In August 2023, India's ISRO agency placed an uncrewed probe in the Moon's south pole region and also showed it had the know-how to return a portion of its delivery vehicle to Earth-orbit—a capability critical for any crewed lunar mission. This remarkable achievement came two days before the Russian space agency's failed attempt to land its uncrewed *Luna 25* probe in the same polar region. (Because the Moon's poles are the areas that receive the most direct sunlight, they have long been considered the most promising sites for a permanent lunar colony of the future.)

Then in January 2024, Japan's JAXA space agency placed its uncrewed *SLIM* probe on the Moon's surface with unprecedented pinpoint precision. Alas, *SLIM* came to rest upside down, with its solar batteries in the wrong position for recharging, thus severely shortening its useful life for data-gathering. One month

This photograph of the Earth, which was captured by the crew of *Apollo 17* as they headed to the Moon on December 7, 1972, was taken from a distance of 28,000 miles. It quickly became a second icon to sit beside *Earthrise* and serve as a companion rallying point for environmentalists around the world. The *Apollo 17* crew chose not to say who had snapped their signature image, which is universally referred to as the *Blue Marble*, preferring that it be known as a work of their collective efforts as space explorers.

after that, US-based Intuitive Machines became the first private company to successfully deploy an uncrewed spacecraft on the Moon. Intuitive's *Odysseus* had a harder-than-planned landing that caused minor damage to the probe. Nonetheless, it was impressive that a privately funded mission had come so close to reaching its ambitious goals.

Other commercial companies have become intensely involved in space exploration. When NASA sends its next crew of astronauts to the Moon, they will be riding atop a giant rocket that is also carrying aloft a lunar landing vehicle designed by SpaceX, the private company owned by Elon Musk. With all this activity in the works and set to continue for the foreseeable future, the Moon appears destined to be a busy place indeed.

Meanwhile, space scientists, engineers, philosophers and futurists like Frank White and Stewart Brand, science fiction writers, and others have all continued to debate the future of space travel. On one side of the argument are those who insist that the time has come to plan in earnest for the day when the Earth will no longer be humankind's primary home planet. Some even believe that such a move beyond the Earth would represent the next giant step in human evolution, and that it is inevitable that cities will one day be built elsewhere in space, whether in the form of permanent settlements on the lunar (or martian) surface, or as orbiting space stations, or in some other as yet unimagined configuration.

On the other side of this argument are passionate environmentalists who remain committed to understanding the Earth's long-term needs and to devising strategies for meeting them, and who continue to be convinced of the importance of keeping the Earth at the center of people's concerns. Among the leaders of this group have been eminent biologists like Lewis Thomas and René Dubos, who envisioned the Earth not as a high-tech flying machine but rather as a living, breathing super-organism capable of sustaining human life so long as the many interwoven strands of its ecosystem are not allowed to get tangled up and destroyed by thoughtless human behavior.

As a result of his *Apollo 8* experience, Bill Anders came to share this view. In his later years, Anders spoke out both to endorse efforts to protect the environment and—especially given the urgency of that need—to question the "imperative," and practical value, of sending humans to Mars, an idea he bluntly dismissed as "almost ridiculous." After his retirement from a distinguished career in government and industry, Anders and his wife, Valerie, launched a foundation to support environmental initiatives as well as projects aimed at "developing tools and technologies to understand, map, and navigate our solar system" and "protect our home planet from asteroid impacts."

Looking back at *Apollo 8*, Anders lamented the fact that "the press and people on the ground" had seemingly "forgotten our history-making voyage." By the 1980s, according to historian Robert Poole, not even all serious environmentalists were aware of the *Earthrise* photo's origins and assumed it had been sent back to Earth by some uncrewed satellite of the distant past. Although *Apollo 8*'s most famous photograph continues to live on as an icon known the world over, Anders believed its meaning could only be fully grasped as part of the larger story of the incredible human effort that led up to its creation.

This was not the first time Anders had bumped up against the false notion that the right machine was capable of accomplishing *anything* that an astronaut could do—at far less cost

The *Apollo 8* mission patch, designed by Bill Anders

to taxpayers. In December 1968, at the final *Apollo 8* prelaunch press conference, Anders had insisted to a roomful of skeptical reporters that sending astronauts into space was worth the price tag and risk for the added dimension of creativity that a team of smart, alert, well-trained individuals could bring to the mission. The enduring power of *Earthrise* shows just how well he and the other astronauts of *Apollo 8* had done their jobs and accomplished their mission.

On April 7, 2024, exactly seven months after Frank Borman's death from a stroke, Bill Anders perished in a private plane crash, leaving Jim Lovell the only surviving crew member. Fifty-six years earlier, in the moments before the famous photograph was taken, Lovell had been about to take sightings of the lunar surface with his onboard sextant. It was his quick work scrambling in the equipment bay for a cartridge of color film and conveying it to Anders that helped the team capture the world-changing photograph.

In 2018, on the fiftieth anniversary of the *Apollo 8* mission, Lovell shared recollections of his thoughts as the crew witnessed Earth from such a startling new perspective:

> *I put my thumb up to the window and completely hid the Earth. Just think, over five billion people, everything I ever knew was behind my thumb.*
>
> *As I observed the Earth, I realized my home is a small planet, one of nine in the Solar System. It is just a mere speck in our Milky Way galaxy and lost to oblivion in the universe.*
>
> *I began to question my own existence. How do I fit in to what I see? Then I remembered a saying I often heard: "I hope I go to Heaven when I die." I suddenly realized that I went to Heaven when I was born! I arrived on a planet with the proper mass to have the gravity to contain water and an atmosphere, the essentials for life. I arrived on a planet orbiting a star at just the right distance to absorb that star's energy—energy that caused life to evolve in the beginning.*
>
> *In my mind the answer was clear. God gave mankind a stage upon which to perform. How the play ends, is up to us.*

BIBLIOGRAPHY
BOOKS

Borman, Frank, and Robert J. Serling. *Countdown: An Autobiography*. New York: Morrow, 1988.

Collins, Michael. *Flying to the Moon and Other Strange Places*, 3rd ed. New York: Farrar Straus Giroux, 2019.

Fishman, Charles. *One Giant Leap: The Impossible Mission That Flew Us to the Moon*. New York: Simon and Schuster, 2019.

Jorgensen, Liisa. *Far Side of the Moon: Apollo 8 Commander Frank Borman and the Woman Who Gave Him Wings*. Chicago: Chicago Review Press, 2022.

Kurson, Robert. *Rocket Men: The Daring Odyssey of Apollo 8 and the Astronauts Who Made Man's First Journey to the Moon*. New York: Random House, 2018.

Mailer, Norman. *Of a Fire on the Moon*. Boston: Little, Brown, 1970.

Markoff, John. *Whole Earth: The Many Lives of Stewart Brand*. New York: Penguin, 2022.

Murray, Charles, and Catherine Bly Cox. *Apollo: The Race to the Moon*. New York: Simon and Schuster, 1989.

Poole, Robert. *Earthrise: How Man First Saw the Earth*. New Haven and London: Yale University Press, 2008.

White, Frank. *The Overview Effect: Space Exploration and Human Evolution*, 4th ed. Denver: Multiverse Media, 2021.

ARTICLES AND ONLINE RESOURCES

NASA's website, NASA.gov, is a treasure trove of primary source material for anyone interested in learning more about the flight of *Apollo 8* and its background. Among the highlights are transcripts of NASA oral history interviews with all three *Apollo 8* astronauts and the transcript of the radio transmissions between Mission Control and the astronauts during the mission itself.

"Address to Joint Session of Congress May 25, 1961." John F. Kennedy Presidential Library and Museum: jfklibrary.org/learn/about-jfk /historic-speeches/address-to-joint-session-of-congress-may-25– 1961

"Apollo 8 Onboard Voice Transcription." NASA.gov (January 1969): nasa .gov/wp-content/uploads/static/history/alsj/a410/AS08_CM.PDF

"Apollo 8: Mission Details." NASA.gov (July 8, 2009): nasa.gov/missions /apollo/apollo-8-mission-details/

Betz, Eric. "The First Earthlings Around the Moon Were Two Soviet Tortoises." Discovermagazine.com (September 17, 2019): discovermagazine.com/the-sciences/the-first-earthlings-around-the -moon-were-two-soviet-tortoises

Bill Anders, quoted in Tom Green, "Sending Astronauts to Mars Would Be Stupid, Astronaut Says," BBC Radio 5 Live (December 23, 2018): bbc .com/news/science-environment-46364179

Brand, Stewart. "'Whole earth' origin . . ." Untitled blog (no date): sb .longnow.org/SB_homepage/WholeEarth_buton.html

Cosmosphere. (April 21, 2023). *NASA video, Earthrise: A Conversation with Apollo 8 Astronaut Bill Anders.* YouTube: youtube.com/watch?v=jrS -LCt9VaY

Dunn, Lauren. "Genetic Similarities Between Dogs and People Are Helping Cancer Research." NBCnews.com (February 10, 2018): nbcnews.com/health/cancer/genetic-similarities-between-dogs-people -are-helping-cancer-research-n841556

"Frank Borman: An Oral History." C-SPAN.org (April 13, 1999): cspan .org/video/?455736–1/radio-american-history-tv-frank-borman-oral -history

Goldstein, Richard. "William A. Anders, 90, Dies; Flew on First Manned Orbit of the Moon." *New York Times* (June 7, 2024, updated June 10, 2024): nytimes.com/2024/06/07/science/william-a-anders-dead.html

"John F. Kennedy Address at Rice University on the Space Effort [September 12, 1962]." Rice University: rice.edu/kennedy

Lovell, Jim. "Apollo 8 Astronaut Remembers Looking Down at Earth." Smithsonian National Air and Space Museum online (December 21, 2018): airandspace.si.edu/stories/editorial/apollo-8-astronaut -remembers-looking-down-earthNASA's Scientific Visualization Studio. "The Story Behind Apollo 8's Famous Earthrise Photo," transcript. NASA.gov (December 21, 2018): science.nasa.gov/resource /the-story-behind-apollo-8s-famous-earthrise-photo/

"Poised for the Leap." *Time*, vol. 92, no. 23 (December 6, 1968), 1–9: content.time.com/time/magazine/0,9263,7601681206,00.html

"Race to the Moon: NASA Wives and Families." *American Experience* (no date): pbs.org/wgbh/americanexperience/features/moon-nasa-wives -and-families/

"Remarks by the President at the National Academy of Sciences Annual Meeting [April 27, 2009]." *The White House, President Barack Obama* online archives: obamawhitehouse.archives.gov/the-press-office /remarks-president-national-academy-sciences-annual-meeting

Sample, Ian. "Earthrise: How the Iconic Image Changed the World." *The Guardian* online (December 24, 2018): theguardian.com/science/2018/dec/24/earthrise-how-the-iconic-image-changed-the-world

"Saturn V Rocket." The Schools' Observatory, Liverpool John Moores University: schoolsobservatory.org/learn/eng/exp/saturnv

Shamberg, Caitlin. "Remembering Yuri Gagarin, Space Hero." *The Takeaway*, WNYC Studios (April 12, 2011): wnycstudios.org/podcasts/takeaway/articles/123666-yuri-gagarin

"Spaceship Earth." (October 19, 2023). *Wikipedia*: en.wikipedia.org/wiki/Spaceship_Earth

"The Fiery Return of the Apollo Missions." *Hack the Moon* blog (no date): wehackthemoon.com/missions/fiery-return-apollo-missions

Tognetti, Laurence. "A Brief History of Soviet and Russian Human Spaceflight." Astronomy.com (May 18, 2023): astronomy.com/space-exploration/a-brief-history-of-soviet-and-russian-human-spaceflight/

Tomaswick, Andy. "The Saturn V Rocket Was Incomprehensibly Loud. Like Thousands of Jet Aircraft Taking Off Together." *Universe Today* (September 8, 2022): universetoday.com/157507/the-saturn-v-was-incomprehensibly-loud-like-thousands-of-jet-aircraft-taking-off-together/

"Vanguard TV-3." (March 17, 2024). *Wikipedia*: en.wikipedia.org/wiki/Vanguard_TV-3

"Vostok 1." (April 2, 2024). *Wikipedia*: en.wikipedia.org/wiki/Vostok_1

"Where Do We Go from Here? [16 August 1967]." Stanford University, the Martin Luther King Jr. Research and Education Institute: kinginstitute.stanford.edu/where-do-we-go-from-here

"Zond 5." (April 9, 2024). *Wikipedia*: en.wikipedia.org/wiki/Zond_5

FILMS

The Apollo Chronicles. Directed by Liz Reph (3 episodes) and Steve Heffner (1 episode), Steve Rotfeld Productions, 2019.

Destination: Moon. Directed by Irving Pichel, Produced by George Pal, 1950.

First to the Moon: The Journey of Apollo 8. Directed by Paul Hildebrandt, Eventide Visuals, 2018.

For All Mankind. Directed by Al Reinert, Apollo Associates and FAM Productions, 1989. *Mercury 13*. Directed by Heather Walsh and David Sington, Netflix/Fine Point Films, 2018.

The Last Man on the Moon. Directed by Mark Craig, Mark Stewart Productions and Stopwatch Productions, 2014.

NOTES

1 THE RACE

p. 10 Because dogs are: Dunn, "Genetic Similarities Between Dogs and People."

p. 10 "Flopnik!"..."Oopsnik!"..."Stayputnik!": "Vanguard TV-3."

p. 14 "I told them": "Vostok 1."

p. 16 "before this decade is out": "Address to Joint Session of Congress May 25, 1961."

2 VISION AND TRAGEDY

p. 18 "We choose to go": "John F. Kennedy Address at Rice University on the Space Effort."

p. 19 Soviet–US competition: Tognetti, "A Brief History of Soviet and Russian Human Spaceflight."

p. 19 became the norm: Shamberg, "Remembering Yuri Gagarin."

p. 22 "These past weeks": Jorgensen, *Far Side of the Moon*, 110–111.

p. 22 "It wasn't discussed": "Race to the Moon: NASA Wives and Families."

p. 24 In 1959, NASA physician William Randolph Lovelace II launched: *Mercury 13*. Directed by Heather Walsh and David Sington.

3 FASTER

p. 35 "human rated": "Saturn V Rocket," The Schools' Observatory.

p. 36 new *Apollo 8* team: Lovell, "Apollo 8 Astronaut Remembers."

p. 37 "Dammit, Borman,": Jorgensen, *Far Side of the Moon*, 142.

p. 37 of their objectives: "Apollo 8: Mission Details."

4 ROCKET MEN

p. 40 At school, he was known as: Kurson, *Rocket Men*, 54.

p. 42 special helmet: *Ibid.*, 143.

p. 42 "Every vision is": Kurson, *Rocket Men*, 85.

p. 45 teased the assembled press corps: *Ibid.*, 98.

p. 46 position could then be calculated: Collins, *Flying to the Moon*, 134.

p. 47 one of the most *un*shakable individuals: Kurson, *Rocket Men*, 93.

p. 47 "How does it feel": *Ibid.*, 145.

p. 47 "These NASA people": *Ibid.*

5 THE NUMBERS

p. 51 A staggering 5.6 million: *Ibid.*, 138.

p. 52 5,000 pages long: Jorgensen, *Far Side of the Moon*, 145.

p. 55 positioning of the space capsule: Collins, *Flying to the Moon*, 36.

p. 55 "putting a letter": "The Fiery Return."

p. 56 "Fifty-fifty": Jorgensen, *Far Side of the Moon*, 149.

p. 56 a one-third chance: Kurson, *Rocket Men*, 43.

p. 56 curious assortment of smaller living creatures: Betz, "The First Earthlings Around the Moon."

p. 57 an elaborate prank: *Wikipedia*, "Zond 5."

p. 59 braced for the worst: Kurson, 104.

6 NO ORDINARY TIME

p. 65 brazen publicity stunt: Poole, *Earthrise*, 133.00 "If our nation": *Ibid.*

p. 65 "an eyeball connected": "Poised for the Leap," 8.

p. 67 taught him the basics: Cosmosphere, NASA video, *Earthrise*.

p. 68 last goodbyes: Kurson, *Rocket Men*, 133.

p. 68 "Mount Marilyn": *Ibid.*, 141.

p. 68 White House state dinner: *Ibid.*, 135.

p. 70 began to spook Borman: *Ibid.*, 140.

p. 70 managed to have a good time: *Ibid.*

7 FIRE AND ICE

p. 73 "You can hear only": Collins, *Flying to the Moon*, 96–97.

p. 75 NASA calculated: Tomaswick, "The Saturn V Rocket Was Incomprehensibly Loud."

p. 76 "like a rat being thrashed": Jorgensen, *Far Side of the Moon*, 167.

p. 76 "slowly, as in a dream": Poole, *Earthrise*, 19.

p. 76 "awesome": *Ibid.*

p. 77 "I mean, let's get comfortable": "Apollo 8 Onboard Voice Transcription," 3.

p. 77 "That was quite a ride": *Ibid.*, 4.

p. 78 fastest-moving humans: Kurson, *Rocket Men*, 167.

p. 78 life vest accidentally inflated: "Apollo 8 Onboard Voice Transcription," 24.

p. 78 scrambling to find: *Ibid.*, 25–27.

p. 78 "We have a beautiful view": *Ibid.*, 41.

p. 79 the fun of life without gravity: Kurson, *Rocket Men*, 209–210.

p. 81 "What I keep imagining": *Ibid.*, 216–217.

p. 83 "We'll see you": *Ibid.*, 227.

8 "LIVE FROM THE MOON . . ."

p. 84 "shards of sunlight": Lovell, "Apollo 8 Astronaut Remembers."

p. 85 "sandpile my kids have been playing in": "Apollo 8 Onboard Voice Transcription," 137.

p. 85 "chattered like excited tourists": Collins, *Flying to the Moon*, 141.

p. 85 the lunar surface: *Ibid.*, 35.

p. 86 critics might accuse NASA: Poole, *Earthrise*, 65.

p. 86 unfortunate result: *Ibid.*, 89.

p. 88 "low-priority photographic subject": *Ibid.*, 24.

p. 89 "Oh, my God": "Apollo 8 Onboard Voice Transcription," 113–114. For audio excerpts of this moment: Cosmosphere, NASA video, *Earthrise*.

p. 90 absolutely sure of it: "Apollo 8 Onboard Voice Transcription," 114.

p. 90 The next few hours: *Ibid.*, 158–167.

p. 91 "Lovell's snoring": *Ibid.*, 165.

p. 91 "This is Apollo 8": Kurson, *Rocket Men*, 260.

p. 91 "whatever's appropriate": "Frank Borman: An Oral History."

p. 91 The crew had used: Poole, *Earthrise*, 133–135.

p. 91 waited almost until the last minute: "Apollo 8 Onboard Voice Transcription," 173.

p. 92 "The moon is a different thing": *Ibid.*, 183.

p. 92 "My thoughts were very similar": *Ibid.*

p. 92 "I think the thing": *Ibid.*, 184.

p. 93 "For all the people": *Ibid.*, 195.

p. 94 "And from the crew": *Ibid.*, 196.

p. 94 "Americans deserved": Jorgensen, *Far Side of the Moon*, 158.

9 THE WHOLE EARTH

p. 95 "Store all the cameras": "Apollo 8 Onboard Voice Transcription," 174.

p. 96 "Please be informed": Kurson, *Rocket Men*, 274.

p. 97 "like a fly": *The Apollo Chronicles*, episode 5.

p. 98 Borman's stomach: Kurson, *Rocket Men*, 304.

p. 101 Within hours, *Earthrise* appeared: *Ibid.*, 315.

p. 104 Brand's prankish lobbying effort: Brand, "'Whole earth' origin."

p. 106 his one-man show: Markoff, *Whole Earth*, 134.

p. 107 "By the way": *Ibid.*, 135.

10 NO PLACE LIKE HOME

p. 108 "a photograph of the Earth": Poole, *Earthrise*, 37.

p. 112 "passengers on a little spaceship": "Spaceship Earth."

p. 113 "I got the feeling": Collins, *Flying to the Moon*, 141.

p. 113 "We came all this way": "Remarks of the President at the
National Academy of Sciences Annual Meeting." Anders is quoted by
President Obama in this speech. The astronaut made this memorable
observation with slight variations in wording on many occasions.

p. 114 Collins himself joked: White, *The Overview Effect*, 243.

p. 114 "Being in Earth orbit": *Ibid.*, 237.

p. 115 "I really believe": *Ibid.*, 241.

p. 116 "Looking back at the Earth": "Frank Borman: An Oral History."

p. 117 "Seeing the Moon up close": White, *The Overview Effect*, 241–242.

p. 117 "not too far": Lovell, "Apollo 8 Astronaut Remembers."

p. 118 "really undercut my religious beliefs": Sample, "Earthrise: How
the Iconic Image Changed the World."

p. 122 debate the future of space travel: Poole, *Earthrise*, 162.

p. 123 "almost ridiculous": Anders, quoted in Tom Green, "Sending
Astronauts to Mars Would Be Stupid, Astronaut Says."

p. 123 "the press and people on the ground": Goldstein, "William A.
Anders, 90, Who Orbited the Moon Aboard Apollo 8, Dies."

p. 125 It was his quick work: NASA's Scientific Visualization Studio.
"The Story Behind Apollo 8's Famous Earthrise Photo."

p. 125 "I put my thumb": Lovell, "Apollo 8 Astronaut Remembers."

CREDITS

Unless otherwise noted, all images are from the NASA archives, available at nasa.gov.

6 US Air Force; 9 Heritage Image Partnership Ltd, Alamy Stock Photo; 13 Arto Jousi, Finnish Museum of Photography, Alma Media, New Finland Collection; 15 Abbie Rowe, White House Photographs, John F. Kennedy Presidential Library and Museum, Boston; 17 National Postal Museum; 20 Marion S. Trikosko, Library of Congress, Prints and Photographs Division; 21 Penguin Random House; 22 ullstein bild Dtl. via Getty Images; 23 Donald Uhrbrock via Getty Images; 27 LBJ Presidential Library photo by Cecil Stoughton; 41 US Air Force; 43 publicdomainreview.org; 46 (top image) Seanavigatorsson Olaf Arndt, Wikimedia Commons; 57 USSR Post; 62 Warren K. Leffler and Thomas J. O'Halloran, Library of Congress, Prints and Photographs Division; 63 Bernard Gotfryd, Library of Congress, Prints and Photographs Division; 64 Warren K. Leffler, Library of Congress, Prints and Photographs Division; 65 Warren K. Leffler, Library of Congress, Prints and Photographs Division; 66 Camera from the collection of the Hasselblad Foundation, photo: Hasselblad Foundation; 70 Robert Knudsen, White House Photo Office Collection, LBJ Presidential Library; 102 (text) *The Beatrice Daily Sun*; 103 Courtesy of the Department of Special Collections, Stanford University Libraries; 104 Library of Congress, Prints and Photographs Division; 105 Courtesy of the Estate of R. Buckminster Fuller; 106 Courtesy of the Department of Special Collections, Stanford University Libraries; 110 National Postal Museum; 111 Courtesy of the Estate of R. Buckminster Fuller; 118 Steve Pyke via Getty Images.

ACKNOWLEDGMENTS

My first thanks go to the history-minded archivists and librarians at NASA who have made a treasure trove of NASA-generated photographs, mission transcripts, and other documentary materials freely available to all online.

Thanks also are due to the following individuals and institutions for responding to my research questions, furnishing needed images, and for offering invaluable guidance as I ventured headlong into largely uncharted territory: Audiovisual Archives Reference, John F. Kennedy Presidential Library; Christopher Banks (Lyndon Baines Johnson Presidential Library); Gail Buckland; Film and Video Collection, New York Public Library for the Performing Arts; Deborah Foley, Andrea Posner-Sanchez, and Lawrence Wong (Penguin Random House); Andréas Hagström (Hasselblad Foundation); Robert Luke Kelly (American Heritage Center, University of Wyoming); Wendell Minor; Tim Noakes (Stewart Brand Archive, Department of Special Collections, Stanford University); Josh Pang (Estate of R. Buckminster Fuller); Public Affairs Office, United States Naval Academy; Linda Schreyer; Charles Simonds; Richard Spencer (Reference Library, NASA); Bruce M. White; and Helena Zinkham (Prints and Photographs Division, Library of Congress).

Working with my superb editor at Farrar Straus Giroux, Wes Adams, his very capable editorial assistant, Hannah L. Miller, and Macmillan's crack copyeditors Linda Minton and Lelia Mander, proofreaders Edmund Mander, Megan Hein, and

Kerianne Steinberg, and indexer Enid Zafran is a rewarding experience as well as a pleasure. I am grateful to them for helping me give this dramatic story its sharpest possible focus and to book designer L. Whitt for having found a way to home in graphically, and with such finesse, on the story's mid-century, space-age vibe.

I thank my agents, Jesseca Salky and Rebecca Altemose, for their thoughtful, patient work on my behalf. And as always I thank my family and friends for their love, encouragement, support, and unfailing good cheer.

INDEX

Photographs are indicated by page numbers in *italics*. Asterisks following page numbers indicate footnotes.